BEFORE YOU START READING,
DOWNLOAD YOUR FREE BONUSES!

Click the link or scan the QR-code &
access all the resources for FREE!

https://dl.bookfunnel.com/h8hzy33mn7

The Self-Sufficient Living Cheat Sheet

10 Simple Steps to Become More Self-Sufficient in 1 Hour or Less

How to restore balance to the environment around you... even if you live in a tiny apartment in the city.

Discover:

- **How to increase your income** by selling "useless" household items
- The environmentally friendly way to replace your car — invest in THIS special vehicle to **eliminate your carbon footprint**
- The secret ingredient to **turning your backyard into a thriving garden**
- 17+ different types of food scraps and 'waste' that you can use to feed your garden
- How to drastically **cut down on food waste** without eating less
- 4 natural products you can use to make your own eco-friendly cleaning supplies
- The simple alternative to 'consumerism' — the age-old method for **getting what you need without paying money for it**
- The 9 fundamental items you need to create a self-sufficient first-aid kit
- One of the top skills that most people are afraid of learning — and how you can master it effortlessly
- 3 essential tips for **gaining financial independence**

The Prepper Emergency Preparedness & Survival Checklist:

10 Easy Things You Can Do Right Now to Ready Your Family & Home for Any Life-Threatening Catastrophe

Natural disasters demolish everything in their path, but your peace of mind and sense of safety don't have to be among them. Here's what you need to know...

- Why having an emergency plan in place is so crucial and how it will help to keep your family safe
- How to stockpile emergency supplies intelligently and why you shouldn't overdo it
- How to store and conserve water so that you know you'll have enough to last you through the crisis
- A powerful 3-step guide to ensuring financial preparedness, no matter what happens
- A step-by-step guide to maximizing your storage space, so you and your family can have exactly what you need ready and available at all times
- Why knowing the hazards of your home ahead of time could save a life and how to steer clear of these in case of an emergency
- Everything you need to know for creating a successful evacuation plan, should the worst happen and you need to flee safely

101 Recipes, Tips, Crafts, DIY Projects and More for a Beautiful Low Waste Life

Reduce Your Carbon Footprint and Make Earth-Friendly Living Fun With This Comprehensive Guide

Practical, easy ways to improve your personal health and habits while contributing to a brighter future for yourself and the planet

Discover:

- **Simple customizable recipes for creating your own food, home garden, and skincare products**

- The tools you need for each project to successfully achieve sustainable living

- Step-by-step instructions for life-enhancing skills from preserving food to raising your own animals and forging for wild berries

- **Realistic life changes that reduce your carbon-footprint while saving you money**

- Sustainable crafts that don't require any previous knowledge or expertise

- Self-care that extends beyond the individual and positively impacts the environment

- **Essential tips on how to take back control of your life -- become self-sustained and independent**

First Aid Fundamentals

A Step-By-Step Illustrated Guide to the Top 10 Essential First Aid Procedures Everyone Should Know

Discover:

- **What you should do to keep this type of animal attack from turning into a fatal allergic reaction**

- Why sprains are more than just minor injuries, and how you can keep them from getting worse

- **How to make the best use of your environment in critical situations**

- The difference between second- and third-degree burns, and what you should do when either one happens

- Why treating a burn with ice can actually cause more damage to your skin

- When to use heat to treat an injury, and when you should use something cold

- **How to determine the severity of frostbite**, and what you should do in specific cases

- Why knowing this popular disco song could help you save a life

- The key first aid skill that everyone should know — **make sure you learn THIS technique the right way**

Food Preservation Starter Kit

10 Beginner-Friendly Ways to Preserve Food at Home | Including Instructional Illustrations and Simple Directions

Grocery store prices are skyrocketing! It's time for a self-sustaining lifestyle.

Discover:

- **10 incredibly effective and easy ways to preserve your food for a self-sustaining lifestyle**

- The art of canning and the many different ways you can preserve food efficiently without any prior experience

- A glorious trip down memory lane to learn the historical methods of preservation passed down from one generation to the next

- **How to make your own pickled goods**: enjoy the tanginess straight from your kitchen

- Detailed illustrations and directions so you won't feel lost in the preservation process

- The health benefits of dehydrating your food and how fermentation can be **the key to a self-sufficient life**

- **The secrets to living a processed-free life** and saving Mother Earth all at the same time

Download All the resources by clicking this link or scanning the QR-Code below:

https://dl.bookfunnel.com/n15biloqb9

BACKYARD HOMESTEADING
&
MARKET GARDENING

2-in-1 Compilation

Step-By-Step Guide to Start Your Own Self Sufficient Sustainable Mini Farm on a ¼ Acre In as Little as 30 Days

Small Footprint Press

Table of Contents

The Backyard Homestead

Market Gardening

"There are no gardening mistakes, only experiments."

— Janet Kilburn Phillips

The Backyard Homestead

Step-by-Step Guide to Start Your Own Self-Sufficient Mini Farm on Just a Quarter Acre With the Most Up-to-Date Information

Small Footprint Press

Introduction

Are you looking for a change? Do you love gardening, or maybe even just like it a little bit but want to take it to the next level? Are you sick and tired of feeling dependent on a system that is becoming increasingly confusing and expensive? Maybe you are just looking to take more control over your own life and want to make the world a little bit better? Well you've come to the right place! Our goal here at Small Footprint Press is to raise awareness about how we all collectively affect the climate and what you can do yourself to make sure you leave the smallest footprint possible on this world.

At Small Footprint Press, we are passionate about helping you return to the land by learning how to take care of Mother Earth and how she can take care of you in turn. We know how important it is to start giving back to the earth and how true happiness can come from living sustainably. That's why we've taken the time to make sure that you feel safe and empowered in your own journey to sustainability. As the world gets more confusing each day, we are determined to keep life simple and ensure that everyone has the ability to survive off their own, homegrown food, no matter what situation they may face.

This book is going to teach you everything you need to know about sustainable living, growing your own food, and good old-fashioned homesteading. Our team has a combined three decades of experience in conservation and land care, and we are ready to pass on our knowledge to you, so that you too can live off the land comfortably and consciously. From personal preparation to prepping your land, understanding preservation, raising animals, and even making a profit, we are here to teach you everything you need to know to start homesteading this season.

The only thing you need to have before you start living sustainably is commitment. Homesteading can be hard work, so it is crucial to make sure you are physically and mentally prepared before you begin. Knowing the obstacles you may have to face as well as the benefits can help you better prepare for the commitment of farming your own homestead. Planning a proper budget as well as finding the right space for your different crops is essential before you *actually* begin any of the real work. This book is going to teach you everything you need to know to get started and prepare you mentally for the tasks ahead.

Once you are ready to start, you also need to make sure your land is ready! Prepping things like garden spaces and structures, fences and pens, even plumbing or irrigation systems will be necessary for certain elements. In order for your homestead to succeed and thrive, you want to make sure you have all the proper equipment and all the right knowledge on how to care for each aspect of your new project. Luckily, we have all the info you need right here, just waiting for someone like you to get started! When it comes to gardening, prepping your space is half the work, which is why we've created this comprehensive guide that will teach you everything you need to know from start to finish.

Here at Small Footprint Press, our number one priority is taking care of the earth, which is why sustainability is so important to us. This guide will consist of all the most up-to-date information on sustainable farming and teach you how to do it yourself. You'll learn all the principles and goals for sustainable homesteading, as well as all the tricks to make sure you are being as environmentally conscious as possible whilst working on your homestead. Homesteading is all about making use of what you have and using everything so that you leave little to no carbon footprint.

After you've grown your crops, though, you're going to need to know how to preserve them. Not to worry; we are here for you once again! On top of teaching the important information on how to prepare and grow your homestead sustainably, we will also provide you with the knowledge of how to preserve your yield. This includes everything from drying and smoking meats, to canning your fruits and veggies, and other options for keeping your produce fresh. There are so many small ways you can live more sustainably by turning common household objects into useful items for your homestead.

Once you get started on your homestead, watch how your life changes for the better; not only directly through the knowledge and pride you will get from growing your own food, but indirectly as well. A sustainable mindset can be applied to every aspect of your life, and we are prepared to help you with that, too. Incorporating animals such as chickens, goats, or even bees can take your homestead to the next level. Even things as simple as an optimized composting system can make your life so much easier and help reduce your impact on our planet.

Finally, we know that tending to your homestead requires a lot of intense effort and that it can take up a lot of your time. That's why we are also going to teach you some tips and tricks for how to profit off of all your hard work! From selling jam and jelly to handmade soaps and lotions to honey and beeswax, our book will give you some great ideas on how your homestead can start working for you, too. You should be able to enjoy all your hard work and have it pay off in a real way that can support you so you can get back to living your best, most sustainable life.

By the time you finish reading, you will have all the knowledge you need to start your own homestead, right in your backyard! Don't stress yourself out by worrying about whether or not you can do it or if you will succeed. Just *try*! There is never success without first failing at least a dozen times, in a dozen different ways. This is especially true when it comes to homesteading. You will only get better through doing, so even when you mess up or make a mistake, keep trying. There will always be new goals for you to reach and new opportunities for you to improve. Homestead-living is all about taking life as it comes, challenges and achievements, hardships and windfalls, obstacles and opportunities.

The No. 1 priority of this book is to help you get the information and tools you need to start living better and more sustainably right now. Our goal is to make sure you are living your best life while helping promote environmental consciousness and eco-friendly initiatives from your own home. Growing and tending to your own personal homestead can be hard work, but it's worth it for the satisfaction and security of being able to provide for yourself. By the time you have finished reading this book, you'll be a theoretical expert, ready to put this knowledge to work and start your backyard homestead!

Chapter 1:

Prepare Yourself

Commitment Is Key

The hardest part about starting your own homestead – or really any project – is committing to it. Ever since I was a little kid, my mom always told me that starting the job is half the work. I've taken this to heart in every aspect of my life, and so should you, because preparing yourself to face any task you may take on is just as important as the work you put into the task itself. When it comes to sustainable living, it is especially important to prepare yourself for the road ahead. Unfortunately, we live in a very fast-paced society and changing your lifestyle to be more environmentally conscious can take a lot of effort. You can do it, though, and once you understand all of the elements that go into creating a successful homestead, you'll be growing your own food in no time.

Commitment is the first and most important step in starting any project, especially one as important as your new homestead. It's one thing to *say* you will start, and do the research, but it is another thing *entirely* to follow through with all the hard work that comes next. We've all had goals that we set and then gave up on, and that's okay. For this homestead, though, you want to make a promise, a commitment to yourself and your future, that you will work hard and make it to the extraordinary payoff.

The key to commitment and follow-through is setting goals. Set big, overarching, long-term goals to look forward to, and smaller, step-by-step goals that you can achieve with some dedicated work. Setting a straightforward and definite goal for yourself will help you to visualize the outcome of all your hardwork. If you start out your homestead just thinking about all the different possibilities, you will be stuck daydreaming forever. Try focusing on one specific aspect of the homestead that you really want to see come to fruition. When challenges arise that you must overcome, go back to your main goal and remember what you are working towards. If you can picture the outcome in your head, you can make it a reality!

Almost as important as commitment is focus. Without focus and direction, your goals will be just that: goals. In order to achieve your backyard homestead, you are going to have to work hard and stay on task. A lot of people tend to struggle with big projects because they get easily distracted, and once you get distracted, it can be hard to return to work. Obstacles and challenges may arise, and there will be roadblocks that you will need to overcome. Without focus, you will get lost in these distractions and find yourself stuck with a half-finished garden instead of a flourishing homestead. When challenges *do* arise, an emotional response can also cloud your judgement, and it may become difficult to see your next steps. Staying focused can help you remember your purpose and the goal you're working towards. Throughout this journey you are embarking on, always remember to go back to the original reasons you decided to start your own homestead and focus on your main goals.

Through focus, commitment, and determination, you can achieve any goal, whether your backyard homestead be a small garden or a vast farm. When it comes to your goals, set large, overarching ones, and plan them out in detail before you begin. When you're in the middle of working, the little things can distract you or stop you in your tracks if you let them. As we've already mentioned, a backyard homestead will require hardwork, meaning it will be tough at times. It's important to not let little setbacks get you too riled up, because with the right efforts, the final product will be *so* worth it. Always keep moving forward, take on one problem at a time, and keep going, even if you feel like quitting. Sustainable living *is* achievable, and once you get through the initial difficulties of focus and commitment, you'll be making huge progress in no time!

Benefits of Homesteading

Why should you start a homestead? The list of benefits is absolutely infinite! There are so many amazing reasons to start your very own homestead. You can grow your own food, raise your own animals, live a more sustainable life, not have to rely as much on outside factors for your resources, and so much more! Homesteading is hardwork, but it can be so rewarding when done properly. Especially living in today's fast-paced world of political and economic turmoil, having your own source of resources can be so important to maintaining your own personal health and happiness. Moreover, the time is now for each of us to start doing our part to heal this earth and help prevent environmental damage that add to the effects of climate change. There are innumerable great reasons to start your own backyard homestead, so in order to prepare you, we want to discuss just a few now to get you motivated and ready to work!

If nothing else, homesteading can provide you with important resources such as food and other plant or animal by-products. It will also teach you the importance of hardwork and build your strength physically and emotionally. Working on a homestead, having to tend to the land and raise plants and/or animals will build such a strong work ethic. It is a big responsibility and commitment, and to make the decision to start your own homestead will teach you so many important life lessons. By growing your own food and creating energy and sustenance for yourself completely from scratch, your outlook on life will be drastically changed and make you a stronger and more well-rounded human being.

Homesteading will also greatly humble you. It can be a difficult process at times, and mistakes show. Forget to water one of your plants on time? The whole thing may die, meaning you have to start again. Crops can die, structures can fall over, etc. Whether it be by accident or mistake, life happens, and homesteading can be frustrating. It's the challenges that make it so rewarding, though, and overcoming these mistakes or obstacles you may face will keep you humble, build your endurance, and make you a better homesteader and person. Keep up your perseverance, focus on your goals, and improve every day; that's how you learn any new skill, and that is what makes life all the more worth living. The sweet reward of successfully cultivating your crops or taking care of your animals will be all the sweeter after you've faced the hardships of the work.

Homesteading also tastes *so* much better. If you're a foodie—or have a very distinguished palate—you can always tell the difference between fresh, locally-grown fruits and vegetables, and the long-haul, prefrozen, store-bought whatever. Same goes for meat from animals. You can taste the difference between naturally-raised, grass-fed chickens vs the stuff you get from factory farming that's pumped full of chemicals and hormones. Food grown organically and locally always tastes 100 times better, and you can be certain that it was grown or raised with love and care. Even if you aren't the kind of person who can normally taste the difference, just knowing that your own hardwork and effort went into creating and preparing the food you eat will make it taste far better.

Homegrown food always tastes the best. My own mother always keeps a garden in her backyard and grows tomatoes, carrots, cucumbers, and more. Each summer, she makes her homemade salsa with fresh tomatoes from her garden, and you can *truly* taste the difference! When she makes it with store-bought ingredients, it just isn't the same. Besides, homesteading will also boost your appreciation of the foods you eat. Knowing how much hardwork you put into making sure your food grows full and delicious will only increase your pride and your joy of getting to eat. Knowing all the effort you put into planting, tending to, and harvesting your crops makes the reward of feasting on it even better than before.

This remains all the more true when it comes to meat. Raising animals for their meat is a difficult process that takes an incredible amount of work and willpower. Raising animals is a lot different than tending to crops and takes even more responsibility and perseverance. When you buy meat from the butcher or the grocery store, you don't have to think about all the hardwork that goes into raising an animal. You think even less about the difficulty it takes to then kill and butcher the animal and prepare the meat for consumption. It takes not only a lot of effort and physical strength, but intense emotional strength and resilience as well. Being the one to raise, kill, and prepare the meat yourself can teach you the true value of what you consume, and it will show you how to be more conscious of what you eat and when.

Homesteading is also such a great teacher of all kinds of life lessons. Obviously, you will learn how to tend to your crops, raise your animals, keep everything running smoothly, etc. But there is so much more you learn. Hard work teaches you perseverance, as we've mentioned; it teaches you about where life comes from, and how precious it is. Tending to your own food teaches you the value of every part of the system; without water or sunlight, your plants won't grow, and without your own input, it can all fall apart. Homesteading will teach you about the earth and its needs, as well as your own needs and your families' needs. You can learn how to prepare your food and cook it more efficiently or in different, delicious ways. The patterns and life cycles of honey bees, turning milk to cheese, water and energy usage, how to gut a chicken, how to perform first aid, etc. All of these things and more can be learned through homesteading and commitment to the craft.

The Homesteading Mindset

Before you can begin working on your homestead, you need to first change your mind, or rather, your mind*set*. In order to live a viable, environmentally-friendly lifestyle, you need to shift your perspective away from consumerism and towards sustainability. This means focusing more on how you can make, remake, or reuse the tools and materials you have at your disposal instead of buying things you may not need. The goal of homesteading is to be self-sufficient and not need to rely on consumerism or capitalism to get you through your day. The first step to living a happier, more peaceful life and becoming more in tune with the earth is to stop thinking about what you need and start thinking about what you already have.

The first step to changing the way you think is to redefine your standards of success. Think about what success looks like to you. If success means making a lot of money, buying expensive clothes and a fancy car, then you have a long road ahead of you. The main goals of your homestead should be security, sustainability, and self-reliance. Once you are able to see these key elements as the standard of success, *that's* when the real change will begin. Success doesn't even need to be measured by productivity, but simply by the effort you are making. If you are working hard, and you can recognize that you are doing your best, then each day will be a successful one on your homestead.

Changing your views of success can be a difficult thing to learn, or rather, *un*learn. Everything we view as successful in modern society is held by the standards of capitalism, meaning that success directly relates to money. As we said before, your homestead is about self-reliance; harnessing your value as an individual, putting your energy into making yourself a better person, and making the world a better place. Once your focus is on the work *instead* of the possible outcomes, that is when you will be able to start your best work.

Another important tip to remember when working on your own personal homestead is to always be prepared to adapt your plan. Sometimes things won't go your way, whether it be by accident, mistake, or just sheer bad luck. You should always keep in mind that Mother Nature is a fickle lady, and her mood will affect your plans. Being able to improve, shift, or adapt your plans into something new when things don't go the way you want is crucial in the homesteading world. Maybe your chickens aren't laying enough eggs or your crops aren't doing too well. Your plans will have to change along with the whims of the planet, and maybe you'll have to start raising ducks instead of chickens or plant different crops for the season. Nothing ever needs to be set in stone, and you should always be open to learning new things.

For many people, even just *starting* a homestead is a brand new area of knowledge, and learning something completely new can be hard, but don't be intimidated. Homesteading techniques and tricks change every season, and people are always coming up with new, better ways to work. Even professionals can learn something new every day. Always be open to trying new things and learning new techniques or habits for your homestead. Instead of facing your failure at something and feeling defeated, focus on ways in which you can overcome your obstacles, even if it's as simple as how you can improve next time around. Learning new ways to find success on your homestead is the most important part of long-term prosperity for you and your homestead.

As we've mentioned, your mindset means everything when it comes to your homestead. Remaining positive in the face of adversity, staying focused on your goals, and using your struggles as fuel to your pursuits is the only way to stay on track and find success. Every obstacle you face in your homestead can be overcome; if not this season, then in the next. Finally, make sure you are open and excited to change. Change will come regardless of the plans you make and hardwork you put in, so always be prepared to change your mindset and your plans to overcome whatever challenges it may bring. Homesteaders must be resilient as well as adaptable, so don't be afraid to fully embrace the adversity, so that both you and your homestead come out the other side stronger.

Your First Goals

The very first part of building your homestead is to set your goals. Obviously, these goals may shift, change, or even grow once you get to work, but setting the initial goals will propel you into the homesteading lifestyle. These first goals should include your budgets, target dates, what crops you will be growing or animals you will be raising, and more. The purpose of these first goals is to give you a good baseline for your homestead planning. Your budget and target dates will determine what you grow and when, as well as give you an idea of what structures or equipment you may need to build or acquire beforehand. While the plan may change as you go, these first goals that you set will be the backbone of your entire homestead, so we want to make sure you are ready and informed for anything and everything!

Sometimes, the process of just *setting* a goal can be overwhelming, especially when you are just starting. Having a clear, set goal is the first step to any plan, though, and completely necessary for any successful project, particularly something as important as a homestead. A properly written goal can guide you through the entire process from start to finish and gives you a determined target for which to aim. A well-planned goal should follow the 'SMART' method, that is, it should be Specific, Measurable, Achievable, Relevant, and Time-bound (Carleo, 2017). Using this criteria, you can ensure that your goals are well-thought-out and prioritize your success.

When you follow the SMART system of setting a goal, you can easily see the steps to your plan unfolding even before you begin. A goal must be 'Specific' enough that success or failure can be easily determined. Your goal should also be 'Measurable'; when it comes to homesteading, your success will be measured in land, yield, time, energy, and even profit. Your goal should take all of these measurements into account. Next up is 'Achievable', which is pretty self-explanatory. Your goal should be realistic in respect to what you have at your disposal and your own capabilities. Next is 'Relevance', and in terms of homesteading, this step is pretty simple.

Make sure your goal is relevant to the work you are doing on your homestead, and make sure that the goal makes sense to follow through in the time and space with which you will be working. Finally, we reach 'Time-bound', which means that you need to set a deadline. A goal without a deadline is just procrastination. Making a deadline will encourage you to work hard and helps you to hold yourself accountable for your own success or failure.

To set a proper goal, you must first determine two things: where you are trying to go and when you want to arrive. Knowing where you start off and where you are aiming to be helps to create a timeline as well as a loose plan for how you will work to achieve your goal. Be specific, and set different goals for each individual aspect of your homestead. The more specificity in your goals, the easier you will find it to follow through. For beginner homesteaders, your first goals should be to learn and prepare yourself and your land. Reading this book is already a great first step to take towards achieving that goal!

Budgeting For Your Homestead

One extremely important thing to keep in mind when planning your homestead is your budget. Especially when you are just getting started, budgeting is an essential part of the homesteading process. Luckily, budgeting for any project always follows similar patterns, so if you've ever had to budget for a big project before now, you already know most of what you will need. Homesteading, like any other project, requires careful planning in regards to spendings, earnings, and budgets. The first stages of building your homestead will require purchasing or building equipment, starters, planters, soil, and much more. Knowing the cost and value of everything you're going to need is crucial as you begin your journey of homestead-living.

The most important part of any good budget is to write it down. Whether it be on paper, online, in an app, or whatever you may choose, get those numbers out of your head and into the physical world. Your mind isn't foolproof, and you will forget things, so keeping track of everything is *crucial*. The second most important part of a budget is research. No matter what you are buying or saving for, always do your research *first*. When it comes to homesteading, maybe you're thinking of raising chickens, in which case you're going to need a coop, feed, and much more. Do your research into the cost of every element you need to purchase, and keep track of all your expenses so you know how much you've put into a project.

When it comes to expenses and budgeting, all projects come with the same tips and tricks to keep you on top of your money. Always know the difference between your wants and needs, and do your research before buying anything important. When it comes to larger purchases, maybe you want to get a tractor to make taking care of your homestead easier; always sleep on it! I find that waking up in the morning with a clear mind gives me new insight into most aspects of life, especially budgeting for the homestead.

Rules and Regulations

One very important piece of research you need to do before starting your homestead is find out about the homesteading laws and regulations in your area. Always check the laws for your region or municipality before doing any construction or land preparation. You don't want to get caught off guard by a surprise visit from a bylaw officer. Knowing the rules surrounding homesteads and farms for your region is crucial to the preparation process.

In the United States, there is what's called a "Homestead Exemption" that is applicable in many states. The "Homestead Exemption" is a legal act that protects homesteaders and has a few different benefits. In most states, you must submit an application in order to qualify for this exemption, so be sure to do your research regardless of where you live. The benefits of this Homestead Exemption relate to property taxes and tax loss reimbursement. Check out more information on your government website for the Homestead Exemption opportunities in your area.

Prepping Your Home

Finally, the last step of the planning process is to prepare your home. Homesteading takes up space, so make sure you clear out anything you don't need around your property that may just be taking up space. You are going to need to be capable of fending for yourself on your homestead, so make sure that the entire area is properly cleaned and ready to go. Whatever space you have, whether it's a large plot of farmland or a small suburban backyard, make sure you clear out as much of the area as possible before you begin. Then, you're going to want to build or set up some sheds.

Building a Shed

Regardless of what kinds of crops you want to grow or animals you want to raise, you are going to need shed space. Whether it be for storing equipment, soil, seeds, extra materials, or any other number of things that may be useful on your homestead, you are going to need a shed or two in your yard to keep it all organized. Not to worry though; building a shed is pretty simple, and if the task seems a little daunting, there are always options for purchasing one and having it installed or even getting a kit with all the components and putting it together yourself.

A simple shed is pretty easy to construct, seeing as it is basically just a large box with a roof and a door. We've already discussed the budget and bylaw aspects you need to consider before building a shed, but you should also consider the weather in your area and the properties of the ground on which you will be building. In my mother's garden, for example, she backs onto a large hill so a portion of the yard is sloped. When I made her a shed to keep her gardening supplies, I had to make it large enough to be useful, but also small enough that it could fit on the side of the yard closest to the house, where the land was flat. If you live in a hilly area, or have a sloping yard where you plan on setting up your homestead, you may need to take some extra steps in building your shed.

The foundation of any building is the first and most important step, so make sure you have a strong foundation that's properly measured before you continue building. If this is your first building project, I recommend closely following a guide from a credible source or enlisting the help of someone who has worked on similar projects previously. If this isn't an option, your local hardware store will likely have all the tools and equipment you need to get started. Don't be afraid to ask the hardware store employees for their advice or help, either, especially when you are a beginner. There are also a number of DIY guides and videos online that detail *exactly* how to build a shed, ranging from a tiny gardening box to a whole barn house, so don't be afraid to watch some tutorials or read a few blogs!

After the foundation, the roof is the most important part of any building. It must be sturdy and strong, but not too heavy so as to put weight on the walls and support structures. Depending on what you use to construct your shed, you may need to use specific roofing materials. Your local hardware store should be able to advise you on this as well, but we would recommend using felt, bitumen roof sheets, bitumen shingles, plastic lightweight roof tiles, or wood shingles to create a sturdy and waterproof roofing to your shed.

Powering Your Homestead

When it comes to power, there are a few different options you may want to investigate before you begin your homestead. Some smaller equipment you'll be working with is battery-powered or electric, and that's fine for the small stuff. You may find, however, that your homestead requires a lot more power than you can justify adding to your electric bill. In that case, you may want to look into solar power options or even erecting a windmill for power storage. This may seem difficult or too far out of your comfort zone, but not to worry; we've got you covered!

Solar power is actually quite simple. Solar panels made up of silicon, photovoltaic cells capture sunlight and convert it into electricity. The electricity can then be used to power just about anything in and around your home. Solar panels can be easily installed onto your rooftop or even the roof of a shed. The panels will generate direct current electricity which must be fed into an inverter to then become alternating current electricity. Then, with the use of a switchboard, you will be able to utilize this electricity wherever you may need. Any unused electricity that your solar panels provide will get fed directly into your city's electricity grid, which also earns you credit towards your electricity bills.

Solar panels can be extremely useful, especially when working on a homestead. After installation, they require little maintenance and provide quality power for a long time. The only components are the solar panels, the inverter, a switchboard, and a mandatory utility meter that your electric company can install for you. Afterwards, you will have power from the sun running all your tools and equipment. If it seems a little complicated, you can always give your local solar power company a call and ask for a consultation. Solar power will help reduce the cost of electricity, provide for not only you but your entire neighborhood by feeding into the power grid, generate backup power for nighttime or outages, and operate efficiently on both small and large scales. It's even environmentally conscious as it takes up very little space and all the energy comes from a renewable resource.

Another option when it comes to powering your homestead is wind turbines. Though they can be expensive to initially erect, wind turbines provide energy at a constant and consistent rate. Definitely do some research on wind turbines and whether this system will be right for you and your homestead. If you live in a residential or urban area, it is likely that you will run into too many conflicts with zoning regulations and local homeowner associations, but if you are in a rural area and have the space, a windmill could be just what you need to complete your eco-friendly, home power system. Even in less than optimal wind conditions, a turbine can easily provide enough power to boost your system. Renewable energy experts often recommend a combination of solar and wind power systems for people looking to live more sustainably or even off-grid.

Life on the Homestead

Now that you're informed, it's time to start working towards building and running your homestead. It will be difficult at first, especially if you are used to living a lazy, comfy life. Homesteading requires effort, determination, commitment, and perseverance. It's completely, 100 percent worth it, though, and while it may be a lot of work, there are so many reasons to get started on your homestead today.

Homesteading will provide you with a better connection to nature and to your food. When you grow and raise your own food, you know it's entire life cycle, from start to finish. You also know *exactly* what goes into making the food you eat, so you never again have to worry about added sugars or salts or even chemical additives that are used in processed foods. Going organic tastes so much better and knowing that it was your own hardwork that went into making something will make it all the more delicious.

Homesteading will also provide you with freedom and security. You are no longer going to need to rely on corporations and big chain grocery stores to provide you with healthy, organic options. By working on your homestead, you will be able to provide yourself and your community with delicious, natural foods for a much better price. You will also have the ability to store and save everything you grow. Homesteading provides you with all the food you could need should you encounter hard times.

Homesteading will change your life forever. Get ready to become a happier, healthier, stronger, smarter, and more rounded version of yourself. It's hardwork, but anything worth it always is. Once you start working on your homestead, you will learn so many new things. Your palate will develop as you eat better, your fitness will improve as you work harder, and even your mood will be better once you start working on something that you know will benefit you and your family. Yes, homesteading will change your mindset and perspective of the world for the better, and it will make you a completely different person. That's a good thing, though! Your homestead will provide for you just as much work as you put into it.

Chapter 2:

Ready the Land

Now that you are mentally prepared, it's time to physically prepare for your homestead! Just like any big project, homestead requires some physical preparation before you *really* begin. You need to clear the space, prep the land, and even figure out some logistics like plumbing and irrigation. You know by now that homesteading is no small task; it's going to take some work, but it'll pay off when you finally get to chow down on that fresh, homegrown produce.

You want your homestead to be as successful as possible, which means that preparation is key. By prepping the area in which you'll be working, you can guarantee that you are giving your crops or animals their best chance to not only survive, but *thrive* this season. Prepping your homestead means working on the land around you, building the structures you may need such as fences or plant boxes, and even plumbing and outdoor wiring. All of these steps are recommended though not necessary, and depending on the size and scope of the land you're working with, you may have to tweak some things or skip some steps to make it work for you. That's totally fine! As long as you're working your hardest and using everything you've got, you'll do great!

Terraforming Your Homestead

Before you can plant anything, you need to lay down some groundwork. Depending on where you live, you may not be able to successfully grow any plants without first using extra soil and fertilizer. That's alright, though, because soil is all around us, and making your own compost is easier than you might think!

Making your own compost is super easy, and it can take your garden game to the next level. Now, the best compost is made with an equal mix of greens and browns. Greens are nitrogen-filled materials like manure, green grass, or weeds. The brown materials, like straw, dried leaves, or wood chips, are all high in carbon. With this winning combination of nitrogen and carbon, you can kick-start your at-home compost system that recycles and reuses any organic material you don't need. The benefits, aside from being environmentally-friendly, are that your compost can be used to fertilize your crops and help them grow bigger, better, and stronger.

Another great trick for your homestead, especially if you don't have much space, is to try dry gardening. Instead of having your crops all spread out, grow them densely together, and plant the roots as deep as you can to encourage stronger growth. From there, water minimally. Though plants need lots of water to thrive, growing them slowly by watering less—or using a drip irrigation system —can make them stronger and more resilient and increase your chances of having them grow back even stronger next season. Dry gardening is especially useful if you live in a more arid climate or to prepare in case of an emergency like a water shortage or a drought. Garlic and potatoes are a couple of great candidates for dry gardening, as they can easily grow closely together and excess water can actually dilute their taste, which you don't want.

If you are going to raise animals, it's extremely beneficial to grow food for them as well. Instead of buying feed, save money and time by planting foods that your animals can chow down on as well. Chickens can eat all kinds of different seeds, such as pumpkin and sunflower, as well as corn, cooked or raw root vegetables, and most of your kitchen scraps. Horses can eat grass from almost anywhere, certain kinds of nontoxic weeds, and even veggies right from your kitchen. Cows and goats are similar and can even eat alfalfa and the leaves off of raspberry plants. Feeding your animals with homegrown food is not only healthier for them as it is all natural, but it also helps with your homestead maintenance. The animals can eat a lot of the 'leftovers' of the food you grow that aren't appropriate or appetizing for humans. If you are going to raise animals, we definitely recommend acquiring a hand scythe to cut grass for feed, as well as growing winter squash, a delicious option that is good for almost all farm animals.

When it comes time to finally plant and grow your crops, aim for a flat and sunny spot. Most homestead crops require a lot of direct sunlight, but this can vary depending on what you are growing and where you live. Crops will also grow best on flat terrain, as sloped or hilly areas can be more susceptible to change and deterioration under harsh weather conditions. Planting something on a hill can also mess with the roots, which ideally grow downwards and outwards. On a sloped surface, the roots may grow at odd angles, affecting the growth of the entire plant.

Garden Structures

There's a few different structures you will almost certainly need to build or buy when starting your homestead. Planter boxes, raised beds, soil blocks, and possibly even some grow lights, are all necessary for the healthy and hearty growth of tons of different plants. Not to worry; all the supplies you need can be easily acquired from a hardware store or garden center, and many of these projects are pretty simple.

Raised beds and planter boxes are the easiest garden structures to build yourself, but you can always buy premade ones from your local garden center. All you need is some planks of wood, some 2x4s, screws, and a drill. Obviously, the sizing is going to depend on how big you want your planter boxes to be, how much space you have/need, and how high off the ground you want your raised beds to be. For these kinds of projects, you can easily get the materials you need and then do the measurements and cuts at home with a circular saw. If you aren't comfortable cutting the wood yourself just yet, do not worry; your local hardware store should be able to do it for you if you request.

The main thing to worry about with planter boxes is proper measurements. You want to ensure that your plants have the best chance to grow and thrive, and that means making sure that their home is in the ideal conditions. Measure twice and cut once, as the saying goes. You don't want to accidentally make one side longer than the other and have your whole garden suddenly growing lopsided.

Another especially helpful tip I've learned from my own personal gardening experience is to layer your planter boxes—especially ones that are raised above ground—with plastic lining and garden fabric before adding soil. Not only does the layering take some of the pressure off the box once you add the soil, but it also helps preserve your planter boxes from water damage when you are watering and tending to your plants. You can easily cut and place a sheet of plastic lining and staple it into place or use screws over the plastic to keep it in place. Don't forget to cut the drainage hole in the bottom of your planter boxes and the plastic lining if you choose to add it. Without proper drainage, your plants may get over watered or the weight of the wet soil will put extra, unnecessary pressure on the planter boxes.

Before you can plant anything in your garden beds, though, you need to grow your seedlings indoors. Growing your seedlings under a glow lamp or even just near a window in your house before planting them outside can really make-or-break your season. Many types of seeds will not grow under harsh conditions, and if you plant them in the ground too early in the year, they will die before they even start to sprout. Using a grow light to grow your seedlings before planting them can promote stronger growth after they are transferred and give them a better chance of surviving and growing strong. Grow your seedlings in small containers or napkins with nutrient-dense soil in greenhouse-like conditions; meaning lots of sun and water. If you don't have a good spot in your house that gets lots of natural sunlight, you can purchase a grow light to help with this.

A great tool that we recommend for beginner homesteaders is a "soil blocker". It is a small tool that takes loose soil and compresses it into tight blocks, just like those that you would get in a seedling tray, only without the excess plastic components. Not only is this method extremely easy and more sustainable as it uses less plastic, but it's actually far more practical than some other methods as well. For instance, using plastic seedling trays can often take up a lot of unnecessary space. These trays are also not optimal for root growth, as the plants grow at different rates and some will outgrow the tray before others have even sprouted. Furthermore, depending on the scope of your homestead, you may not need a full tray of certain seedlings, meaning that half a tray is just empty and taking up space. With the soil block method, you can make as many soil blocks as you need, and they are much easier to transfer into your garden when the time comes.

Another project you may want to include in your homestead is an arbor or trellis. These are beautiful decorative pieces but can also be extremely useful if you are growing vines or other plants that may need a structure to help them stay upright when they grow. Beans, peas, cucumbers, and even summer squash and some types of melons need a trellis or ladder structure to help them remain upright while they grow to fruition. The type of trellis you need will vary depending on what you are growing, but a basic trellis can be made with a couple of wooden posts and some twine. For something a little sturdier, try using chicken wire and attaching that to the wooden posts instead. If you want to go a bit fancier, there are many arbor and trellis options that you can purchase online or at a garden center, or you could build your own by following one of the many DIY's available for free online.

Fences

The next structure you're going to need on your homestead are some fences. This will be particularly useful when it comes to raising animals, as you will need to learn how to build and repair the animal pens. We'll talk about raising animals a little later in Chapter 5, but for now, let's focus on getting these fences set up. Whether it be a picket fence to surround your garden or a sturdy gate to keep wild animals off your land, strong fences are essential for any homestead.

The first step to building a fence is to set up the fence posts. If you don't set the posts up properly, the efficacy of the entire structure will be compromised. When putting up a fence post, you first want to dig a hole in the dirt where you'll be placing it about 12 to 18 inches deep. You can choose to go shallower or deeper, but this is the depth we recommend to ensure a sturdy and robust post. The reason you need to dig so deep is that you are going to want to fill the hole with cement when you put the post in the ground. This is to create a strong foundation for the entire fence. You can also choose to add a couple inches of peat gravel at the bottom of the hole before you put in the cement and fence post. This will block the wooden post from resting directly against the earth and therefore protect it from any deterioration. Dirt and soil can easily rot wood after prolonged exposure, especially in moist conditions like that of a garden or homestead, so this step is vital to the durability of your fences.

When you first set up your fence post, be sure to check that it is level before anything else. Double check after you've added the cement mix, and then *triple check* it after the cement has had time to harden and solidify. Once you are absolutely certain that your fence post is upright and sturdy, *that's* when you should proceed with the rest of the fence. The type of fence you are building will dictate your next move. You may want to add metal braces if you are looking to build a larger, stronger fence. For something small and simple, though, you can easily just connect the horizontal planks directly to your fence post. This is also a great way to make a homemade trellis or arbor; just add a cross beam at the top and bottom of your fence posts, and add twine, string, chicken wire, or whatever other material you may be using.

One way to easily set up a long fence is called 'stretching'. This method is especially useful for large field fences that are very long and would take a lot of time to set up each individual section. It works by rolling out wire fencing along a long, straight stretch of fence posts and then putting it all up at once. What you need for this method is your already-installed fence posts and a large roll of chicken wire or other wire fencing. First, attach one section of wire fencing to your initial two fence posts. This must be done after you've put in your 2x4s—or whatever wood you may be using—for structural support. You can use a staple gun to keep the wire fencing connected and then add nails as you see fit for structural integrity.

Now, using the rest of your roll of wire fencing, lay it on the ground, and unroll it along the straight length of all your fence posts. The wiring should only be attached to the very first two fence posts and line up on the ground next to the rest of the fence line from there. Make sure it is in a straight line, flat on the ground, and even. Once that is done, you are going to use a metal 'T'-post, and weave it through the wire fencing at the end of your straightaway. This is going to be your come-along; the part that holds everything together. It should also be placed only a few feet past the final fence post. From here, you are going to attach the 'T'-post to the bumper of a truck, car, tractor, or any other strong motorized vehicle using some metal chains. Then, very carefully and gently, use the vehicle to pull the entire length of the wire fencing up against your fence posts. If done correctly, the wire fencing should stand up vertically and pull against the fence posts due to the tension from the first fence post being pulled by the vehicle. Make sure you go slow and steady so as not to break anything or move it out of place. Keeping the line taut, make sure your vehicle is turned off and head back out to your fence. The wire fencing should all be upright against your fence posts now, minus the last one which was attached to the vehicle.

You can now go back along your fence line and attach the wire fencing to all of the posts using staples, nails, wire-wrapping techniques, or whatever other method you may find works best. If you are using metal fence posts throughout the length of your fence line, we recommend getting little wire fence clips that attach on either side of the metal post and keep the wire fencing upright and connected to the fence post. All you need to apply these clips is a pair of pliers to wrap them tightly around the wire fencing for security. Once your wire fencing is fully connected to each fence post, you can head back to your vehicle, reverse slightly to slacken the chains, and release the tension, and then remove the chains from your come-along post. From here, you can remove or leave the come-along post to your liking, as long as the last fence post in the row, prior to the come-along piece, is a sturdy wooden post with a crossbeam for support. If you have more long stretches of fencing (for example, if you are enclosing a large field for horses or cows), repeat these steps on each straightaway you have in your fence. Now your wire fence is complete!

To build a picket fence is a little different because it is a much smaller structure. You will still need to use a similar method of putting up the initial fence posts, including digging a deep hole and adding cement to keep it locked in place for a long time. Place your fence posts no more than eight feet apart, otherwise your 2x4s won't fit properly. Just like how you would for a regular fence, you are going to want to attach a metal brace to hold your 2x4s properly. For the best results and the sturdiest fence, you should have one 2x4 near the top of the fence posts and one near the bottom. This will ensure that your fence is properly supported once you start adding the pickets. Once your fence posts are all connected, it's time to get started on the pickets. You can purchase specific wood for picket fences at a hardware store or make your own using 1x6 fence boards and cutting them to your desired length. Cutting these boards yourself will take some extra time, but can also save you some money. Don't forget to cut off the top of the boards in a 45 degree angle on either side to make a nice, pointed tip to your picket fence.

When it comes time to attach the pickets to your fence, it can be a little tricky to get the spacing right without a proper guide. Using one of your pickets, you can make a guide by attaching a spare block of wood to the top right above the level at which the upper 2x4 is attached. Then attach another, slightly longer block of wood to create a sort of hook that can be easily placed over the upper 2x4 of the fence and pushed along the length of the 2x4. By doing this, you effectively create a spacing guide for your picket fence. Screw on the first picket, then use your guide by placing it right up next to the newly-installed picket. Attach your second picket on the other side of the guide you built, and when you remove the guide, the two pickets will be perfectly spaced. Repeat this process across the rest of your fence as you continue to add the pickets to ensure that they are all evenly-spaced. The spacer guide that you've created will ensure that everything is evenly-spaced and uniform across the entire fence. Now that your fence is built, all that's left is to paint it whatever bright and vibrant color you want!

Now, you can always hire someone to come in and help install a fence for you. However, installation is generally charged per foot of fencing, which can get pretty pricey. Building your own fence is always going to be the cheaper alternative. Especially if you are planning on raising animals and are going to need multiple fences of different sizes and styles, it is always better to do it yourself if you feel confident. There are so many free resources and guides available online to help you if you get lost along the way, and the rewarding feeling of completing a project on your own will be so worth it. Plus, all the money you will save on installation fees won't hurt, either.

Depending on where you live, you may want to consider a solar-powered electric fence. An electric fence can be extremely beneficial at protecting your animals and crops from local predators, such as coyotes, wolves, or even bears. If you have the space and live in a region where these animals are common, you may want to consider it, and using solar power to run your electric fence will keep you off-grid and eco-friendly. An electric fence provides a low-damage shock to any animals, domestic or wild, that touch it. This keeps wild animals out and your own domestic and/or farm animals in check and away from the edges of your property where they may try to run off or get lost. An electric fence often needs a power source, however, and having outlets in the great outdoors is not really an option. That's why solar power is the best way to go and has so many more benefits. The cost of installing an AC power unit, especially if you live in a rural area, and installing one yourself can be dangerous if you don't know what you are doing. Using a solar power charger to power your fence instead is much simpler and can save you a ton of money. Solar power saves you money on electrical bills and can keep your homestead running in the event of a storm or power outage using the stored, backup energy it has saved after many days of sun exposure.

Gates

The most important part of a fence is a good, strong gate.

If you make your fence all the way around in a perfect square, how are you going to get in and water your crops or feed your animals? Whenever you build your fence, remember to leave an open space at some point to insert a gate; otherwise, you are going to have to do some intense climbing or jumping every time you want to get inside! Building a gate for your fences is easy once you've put up the entire fence because it is the equivalent of one small section and is basically just a fence on hinges.

To build a gate, you are going to need almost all the same materials you used to build your fence, plus some metal hinges and a gate lock or handle of some sort to use when you want to open and close it. Once again, you can always purchase a gate and install it or you can build one yourself. Building it yourself is always going to be cheaper, though more time-consuming, so it's up to you to decide what's worth it for your situation.

The most important thing about building your own gate is to make sure it is structurally sound. This means that you are going to want to double-layer it in a way, basically sandwiching your support beams between two 2x4s on either side. To start your homemade gate, cut four pieces of wood—we recommend 2x4s—to the desired length that will be the height of your gate. Remember that this does not mean the same height as your fence, as the gate is going to be off the ground and also may not need to be the full height of your fence, depending on what it will be used for in the end. You will also need to cut three pieces of wood to your desired gate length and a final diagonal piece that will be used for structural support. This last piece can be cut out after you've constructed the gate so that you can double check the length.

When you put the gate together, place the three crossbeams you cut down on top of two of the side beams, creating two equal windows of space. These three crossbeams are your upper, middle, and lower support pieces to your gate. Once you've screwed them together, measure out and cut a square of wire fencing to attach. Make sure you attach the wire fencing directly to the three crossbeams which will be on the inside of the gate. After that, place the last two wood planks over top of the rest of the gate, attaching them to the original two planks that mark the length of the gate. This will sandwich in your crossbeams and wire fencing, ensuring that they won't slip or easily come apart. This step is crucial in making sure your gate will be sturdy and long-lasting. Finally, measure the length from one corner of your gate to the opposite corner, and cut a final plank of wood to that length. Make sure that you cut the ends at a 45 degree angle so that they fit to the gate properly.

Now that your gate is fully built, you need to attach the hinges. Depending on how large your gate is, you may need to buy larger or smaller hinges in order to hold up the weight of the gate. When attaching the hinges, you most likely only need two: one at the top and one at the bottom. However, if your gate is larger and heavier, three may be necessary to ensure structural integrity. Once the hinges are on, get someone to help you hold your gate in place while you make a mark on your fence post one inch below the spot where each hinge will connect. Then, you are going to attach the other piece of the hinge to your fence post, and attach the gate. Make sure that when you attach the gate to the fence post, you are attaching so that the diagonal beam across your gate is at the bottom corner where the hinge will connect. You want the diagonal beam to be leaning towards the opening of the gate as it will help keep the gate robust and sturdy for longer. After that, all that's left is to screw on whatever handle or opening mechanism you are using to the other side of the gate. Again, make sure the handle is in the same upper corner as the diagonal cross plank to ensure maximum structural integrity.

Plumbing and Wiring

The last part of your homestead you're going to need to set up is outdoor plumbing and wiring, as needed. It is absolutely crucial to the success of your homestead that you have a good irrigation system for your crops and a properly built and well-functioning electrical circuit for anything you may need to use electricity for while you work. We are going to cover the basics for outdoor plumbing and electrical wiring; however, you may need a little less, a little more, or a little different depending on your homestead. Remember, whatever works best for you is best for your homestead!

Low-Tech Plumbing

Now, low-tech plumbing isn't for everyone, but if you are looking to save money on your water bill while maintaining a full homestead in need of crop irrigation and water for animals, you may want to try it out. One of the easiest ways to acquire water for your homestead is rain catching. Especially if you live in a region with a rainy climate, collecting rainwater and using it for irrigation is a simple and easy way to save money and time. Obviously, when it rains you won't need to water your crops, but you can save extra water in rain catchers and store it in barrels or bins until you need it. This method can also be used to obtain drinking water for yourself and your animals; although, you have to be sure to purify the water before you consume it. You can do this by getting a water purifier, a purifying solution that can be added to rainwater to cleanse it or go the good old-fashioned route and boil rainwater before consumption. Purifying the water before you drink it is extremely important, as water from anywhere can be contaminated with all kinds of germs and pathogens of which we may be unaware.

Another method for obtaining water is to tap a natural spring or underground aquifer. Tapping a nearby spring or stream is simple enough to do with a hose and spigot. Underground water is a little more complicated and will likely require some sort of well or piping. This is extremely difficult to do yourself, so we don't recommend it unless you have a professional on hand to assist. However, if you live on an old homestead that you are fixing up, you may want to scout around the property as there is likely already an old well that can be restored. If you live nearby a lake or river, you can also try to tap those in a similar fashion to a small stream, however it may be more difficult as you must factor in currents and waves, as well as marine life. Regardless of where you are getting your water, make sure you are purifying and desalinating, if necessary. While it may not be bad for crops to drink up natural water from anywhere, you and your animals have a more complex digestive system, and dirty water can be a serious danger.

Outdoor Wiring

Outdoor wiring can be tricky, but it doesn't have to be difficult. Depending on what you need to power, you may not even need to do much work. First and foremost, check the regulations for your area to make sure that any permits you may require are in order before you start the project. Some places are very strict or specific about outdoor wiring or connecting your house's electrical supply to an outdoor shed. You are also going to want to figure out what works best for you: above ground cables or underground wiring. Underground takes more work to set up, but is generally more stable and less likely to have any problems arise. That being said, if you do face electrical problems with underground cables, it is a lot harder to fix as you may have to dig the entire thing up again.

If you are going to need electricity for a lot of different things on your homestead, we recommend setting up an electrical shed where you can house any equipment or machinery that may be necessary. For example, you can set up a power inverter and storage unit, as well as a switchboard in a small shed to make optimal use of your outdoor electric system and protect the machinery from environmental elements. If you only need electricity for simple things like outdoor lighting, don't worry so much about needing an entire shed. For that, you may just want to run some cables out and set up some lights or lampposts in central areas.

Regardless of what you may be using outdoor electricity for, always consult a professional if you are unsure about something, and make sure you have all the necessary tools and supplies to complete your project before you begin. The last thing you want is to have loose cables or tools lying around while you run to the store to pick up something you forgot. That is an accident just waiting to happen. As with most of the projects we've already discussed, outdoor wiring is something you can hire a professional to do for you, although it is often a lot cheaper to do it yourself. That being said, electricity is not something you want to be messing around with if you haven't studied up on it first. Make sure you know *exactly* what your plan is and what safety measure to use before you start working.

To bury your wires underground and use the underground method of setting up your outdoor electric wiring, you are going to need an underground feeder cable. This is a specialized type of cable that you run the wiring through before burying what protects from any possible damage to both the wires and the environment. Always check the regional guidelines or talk to an inspector about how deep your cables need to be run under the ground before you bury them. It is also important to have flexible conduits that you can easily insert or remove the wires from once buried. This will prevent you from needing to do any extra labor once the project is finished. You can use plastic tubing or PVC piping for this as it is sturdy and has adjustable joints that can be attached for proper direction. Always have an inspector or professional double-check your work before you bury your cable to ensure that it is done properly and safely. Once your wiring is all set up. You can connect it directly to whatever needs power, such as your lights, or you can connect it to a circuit board.

Chapter 3:

Growing Crops the Sustainable Way

The first step to running your sustainable homestead is to understand sustainable agriculture and how to grow crops responsibly, without harming the environment. The trick to a good homestead is to use everything you've got to the fullest extent. This means recycling old materials, repurposing junk to give it new life, and reducing your carbon footprint and environmental impact. The goal of sustainable agriculture—or in our case, sustainable homesteading—is to meet all of your present food and textile needs without harming the environment and the potential for the future. At every step of the process, there are ways we can be more environmentally conscious and make better decisions for the future of our planet.

Homesteading in itself is already a great way to live more sustainably, as you will not have to rely on corporations and industrial agriculture to fulfill your needs. You directly impact your patch of land by caring for it and tending to the plants and animals around you. You also indirectly impact so much more by running a homestead that you may not even realize. The more people who participate in homesteading and sustainable farming, the less need there will be for industrial agricultural practices that pollute the air and the earth in countless ways.

Furthermore, any excess you may produce on your homestead can easily be given back to your community, whereas industrial agriculture is always producing in excess, leaving Mother Nature to take care of the dirty work.

One great way to ensure that you are farming sustainably is to grow the specific foods you may need. While you may be inclined to just go crazy and grow whatever you can, you should be wary of overproduction and overcrowding on your homestead. The human body is a complex system that requires many specific nutrients, vitamins, and minerals. Feed your body and keep your homestead neat by growing foods that are necessary for your health and wellness, without overproducing what you don't need. Growing foods such as squash, potatoes, broccoli, spinach, kale, and peppers is a good start as all of these delicious vegetables contain many of the necessary vitamins and minerals your body needs every day.

We've already discussed setting up a good compost system on your homestead, and this is just another great way to be a little more sustainable in your life. A good compost system can be fed pretty much any organic scraps and leftovers to create nutrient-rich fertilizer for your crops. One great composting tip is to introduce worms into your outdoor compost. Worms eat up organic materials and work to improve production of fertilizer for your homestead.

What to Grow on Your Homestead

At first, it can be difficult to decide what crops you should grow. Before you plant anything, make sure you are aware of the soil conditions and weather patterns in your area. A lot of crops require specific conditions in order to truly thrive on the homestead, so you don't want to start planting a bunch of randomly chosen seeds and do all the work to tend to them only to find out they won't grow due to environmental conditions that are out of your control. There are a lot of crops, however, that are *extremely* hearty and can grow in many different soil and weather conditions. These are going to be your essentials; the crops you *absolutely need* to have on your homestead. After you have the essentials, you can grow to your liking whatever else you may choose, but these crops are the ones we recommend.

Essential Crops

There are some crops that are just absolutely essential to have on your homestead. These fruits and vegetables are considered essential parts of any good garden, as they are hearty, nutrient-dense, and keep for a long time. These crops can save you in the event of a crisis and be delicious additions to your plate if not. They are easy to grow in a variety of different conditions, store well even without electricity or power, and are jam-packed with important nutrients to keep you strong and healthy.

The first is potatoes. The heartiest of foods, potatoes grow underground as root vegetables and are full of starchy, complex carbs that are healthy for you, and they can last a long time in storage. Potatoes actually produce more carbohydrates per square foot than any other vegetable that grows in the US. They are super easy to grow, can adapt to almost any soil conditions, and can withstand harsh weather conditions like rain or storms, unlike many other vegetables. They can also easily be stored without any power or electricity necessary for long periods of time. In some countries, potatoes are even grown without any irrigation.

Next up is corn, the most feasible of any grain product to grow successfully on a small homestead. It is rich in vitamins B_1, B_5, and C, contains minerals such as phosphorus and manganese, and also is dense in nutritional fiber. Grown in the summertime, this grain can also be easily stored during the cold months. It is perfect for hearty, starch-based sides such as corn bread or polenta, great for accompanying fresh meat from your homestead.

Beans, peas, and lentils are all super easy to grow and very nutritious. They are rich in protein and many other vitamins as well. Legumes are also quite easy to store without power or electricity, and different species of legumes can thrive in all sorts of different conditions. We recommend growing a variety of different types of beans and peas, and see what works best for you. You can grow several different species in a relatively small space as well.

Finally, squash. All kinds of squash are great, but winter squash specifically includes gourds such as pumpkins, butternut squash, acorn squash, and many varieties of spaghetti squash. These delicious veggies are quite fruitful (pardon the pun), and though they take up a lot of garden space, the yield is almost equivalent. Winter squash is also much easier to store and keeps for much longer than their summer counterparts. You can display your gourds on your mantle or around the house until it's time to eat, and they will taste as good as ever.

These crops are your basic homestead essentials, but obviously, you can and *should* grow more if you have the space. Carrots, cabbage, spinach, onions, tomatoes, garlic, and asparagus are all great candidates for a successful homestead. Many of the crops are a lot easier to grow than you may think and can yield quite a bit, especially tomatoes and leafy greens such as lettuce and cabbages. Where you live can really affect the crops you are able to grow, so do some research before you plant anything. Finding out what type of plants will thrive in your region can save you a lot of work you would have otherwise put into growing a crop that may not even be able to survive the soil or weather conditions of your homestead.

Best Crops for Your Homestead

While all the essential crops we've gone over are some of the best things to grow, there are some that may be a bit more region-specific—or harder to grow—that are also very good to have on your homestead if you can swing it. The best crops are ones that are nutrient-dense, very hearty, store well, and most importantly: taste delicious!

We've already talked a little bit about corn, but to go into some more detail, you may want to try growing heirloom corn. Instead of just the sweet corn you may be used to, different varieties of heirloom corn can be useful for different situations. There are six types of corn altogether: sweet, popcorn, flint, flour, dent, and waxy. All of these have different conditions in which they thrive and different distinct properties that may be more or less suited to your homestead. Flint corn, for example, grows in cooler, wetter climates, and flour corn is usually grown in the southwest, where it is hotter and dryer. Dent corn is the common field stuff that you are probably used to seeing. It is the easiest to grow and store, and the type we referred to earlier in the chapter. Sweet corn is great to grow in the summer; a delicious addition to any barbeque. However, it doesn't store well and must be eaten or preserved after the initial harvest. It is up to you to decide which variety will work best for you, and this will depend on your environmental conditions as well as your personal preferences and your homesteads capabilities.

We've also already discussed potatoes and their many benefits, but we haven't yet talked about other root vegetables. Radishes, beets, carrots, and many more are all very hearty crops that are generally fast-growing due to their nature. Because these root vegetables grow underground, they often produce more than you'd expect and grow quite fast. Radishes are especially good as you can eat both the purple-red root and the leafy green top to this vegetable. Using the entire vegetable in your meal means less waste as well!

Another group of plants we recommend is herbs and spices, if the climate allows. A simple herb garden can thrive in such a small space and provide tons of fresh, delicious flavor to your home. Chives are notoriously easy to grow, and they will resprout each season with almost no work. Basil, cilantro, mint, and rosemary are also great candidates for your herb garden. Keep these in a small space with lots of sunlight and give them lots of water, but be careful not to overwater them. Parsley and dill also grow fast and fruitful and are great for adding to marinades and brines.

Growing certain types of flowers on your homestead can also be quite beneficial. Though they may not be edible, planting flowers with pollen that attracts honey bees is a great way to help grow your plants stronger through the natural process of cross-pollination from the bees. Attracting bees to your homestead will allow them to thrive in their bee community, and the pollen they drop as they fly through can strengthen the growth of certain other plants on your homestead. Also, growing sunflowers is especially good for homestead-living, as they not only attract bees but also provide you with sunflower seeds. These seeds, along with grains from your corn and other crops, can be used as bird feed if you are raising chickens and are also good for other plant-eating animals that may be on your homestead.

Easiest Crops for Your Homestead

Most of the crops we have already mentioned are pretty easy to grow. Potatoes and other root vegetables like winter squash; really all the essentials are not going to be too tough. We know that you are just starting off your homestead, however, and you may be looking for some other easy crop options that will grow well and don't require too much work while you get settled and figure out homestead life. Not to worry; there are so many options available and so many hearty crops that grow in any conditions. You will be moving on to fancy, complicated farming techniques in no time. Meanwhile, here are some of the easier crops to grow on your homestead that we recommend.

One great opportunity is peanuts. These legumes are

relatively easy to grow and thrive in warmer climates, but can survive in the cold as well. They are also home to nitrogen-fixing bacteria that can keep up the fertility in your garden. Peanuts are full of protein and easy to store, plus they are a delicious snack—great for any occasion!

Another crop you may want to check out is quinoa or amaranth. Closely related to rice, these grains are protein-dense and basically grow like weeds. Once you plant them, they will sprout up everywhere. Quinoa is better for colder climates while amaranth thrives in warmer areas, so you can try your hand at either depending on where your homestead is situated.

Red raspberries are a delicious summer treat that can serve so many purposes: eaten fresh, preserved in jam, or baked into pastries. You can even add the leaves to your salads or brew them into a delicious tea that can relieve some muscle pain and cramps. They grow wild with little care in the summer and warmer season, and they sprout up little shoots that can be dug up and transplanted easily. Thus, you can save your crop for the next season and even replenish or increase your yield with minimal effort.

Another delicious berry you can try your hand at is strawberries. Similar to raspberries, these little guys grow wild and have so many benefits. Strawberry plants are usually the first to sprout in the springtime, providing you with much needed vitamin C. Strawberry plants even have some medicinal properties and can be brewed into tea that can relieve digestive issues such as diarrhea. They are perennial, and each year, they send out runners so that the patch can easily be replenished every season.

On the topic of medicinal plants, Aloe Vera is another great one to grow. Being a common house plant, it can survive in many conditions as long as it is properly looked after and thrives in warmer climates. Aloe Vera also has many healing properties, specifically for skin as the inside contains a gel-like substance that is great for cooling and pain-relief on rashes and burns. Aloe plants are constantly shooting up clones to repopulate that you can transplant, and it requires little watering or fertilization.

Optimizing Your Crop Growth

Regardless of what crops you are growing, optimizing your system is so important for a successful homestead. You want to be able to use your space and resources wisely and with as little waste as possible. Being a sustainable homestead means making use of all your resources and leaving little leftover that goes unused.

There are a lot of different ways to optimize your homestead, especially when it comes to crop growth. One key example is crop placement. There are many plants that you will be growing on your homestead that can do better or worse depending on what is around them. Whichever plants you choose to grow, do some research into which other plants are compatible. It is possible that planting two crops next to each other can form a symbiotic relationship in which both are mutually benefiting from each other's close presence.

It is also important to understand hydroponics and aquaponics so that you have a successful irrigation system in place. Your plants need to be well-watered, without going overboard. You don't want to overwater as it can ruin your crops, and it is a waste of a natural resource. You also don't want to be underwatering and let your crops dry out and die, however, so it is important to know exactly how much water to be giving each of your plants and how often, as well as what system works best for your homestead.

Hydroponics

Hydroponics is a way of growing your crops without soil and instead using a liquid solvent. There can be many benefits to hydroponics, and you may want to consider using this technique on your homestead. At home, hydroponics is not as complicated as it sounds, and depending on how much space you have for your homestead, it may be the right method for you.

Hydroponics uses a mineral, nutrient-dense solution that can come from many different sources to grow crops completely without soil. Many plants such as tomatoes, peppers, cucumbers, and lettuces can be easily-grown hydroponically, clearing up space outside for other crops you may be growing. There are many advantages to hydroponic farming, including the notable decrease in the amount of water necessary. This makes it possible to grow crops in harsh conditions where you may not have access to as much water.

To create a hydroponic system, we recommend you first set up a greenhouse, although it is not necessary. There are a few different ways to set up a hydroponics system at home, and you may need to adjust some of these parts to suit your homestead. For the most part, all you need to create your own at-home hydroponics system is a table or wooden stand on which you will grow your crops, waste pipes to house the water, PVC pipes to connect them together, and a hose with a pump to keep the running water flowing through the pipes. You will also want a large container for the storage of output water. The only other elements you will need are fresh water, oxygen, root support, nutrients, and lots of light.

First, set up the space where you are going to grow your crops. Then, fill a large storage bin with water and mineral nutrient solution. This is what your plants will use to grow strong. Next, using a drill with a rotary circle cutter or hole saw drill bit, cut three inch holes through your waste pipe at approximately seven inches apart. Make sure that the holes you cut are all straight and even on the pipe, as this is where your plants will grow up once the system is in place. Set up your waste pipes on a flat surface in rows. How many rows and how long they are is up to you and will depend on the space you have on your homestead. Once they are laid out, you can use PVC pipe to connect the waste pipes on the end. Make sure all of them are connected in a way that will create one long tube essentially which the water can flow through. At one end, you will insert your hose where the fresh, nutrient-rich water will flow through the entire system. At the other end, you have a tube that drains the water back into the storage bin to be reused.

For a hydroponics system such as this one we recommend, you get a fountain pump that can run continuously without needing to be turned on or off. Connect it to the hose to push the water through your pipes and make sure that your output hose is secure to the water reservoir. You don't want to go out to check on your crops and see that they've all dried up because of a misplaced hose.

Aquaponics

Aquaponics is a step past hydroponics, which combines your water-based, soilless crops with aquaculture; or the raising of fish and other marine life. Aquaponics works to use both fields in a symbiotic relationship to enhance your crops' growth and improve the conditions of the fish. If you are thinking of rearing fish on your homestead, I highly recommend using aquaponics to not only improve the system, but also to save space and optimize the growth of your crops and animals on your homestead. Growing fish and vegetables together is more complicated, as it does involve more moving parts and living creatures to care for, but if you have the time and space, it is worth it.

Luckily, if you understand hydroponics, you are pretty much halfway to aquaponics already. The only difference on the vegetable side of things is that instead of a small storage bin water reservoir, you are going to need a big space where you store your water as that is where your fish will live. As you take care of your fish, they will supply the water with important nutrients that are great for vegetation growth, just like in nature. Aquaponics also relies on a closed system of water, so there is no runoff or waste of any kind.

There are so many benefits to aquaponics for both you and your homestead and its reduced environmental impact. An aquaponics system can cut down so many garden chores, as it eliminates watering and weeding completely. It also saves space in the long run as a small aquaponics system can replace a large plot of land that would be needed to grow your crops. It is a completely natural ecosystem with no added chemicals or pesticides and can be set up almost anywhere. An aquaponics system is also scalable, and you can have a smaller or larger setup depending on how much space you have on your homestead.

The only part of aquaponics we haven't been over is caring for your fish. Just like any plant or other animal, you will have to take care of your fish and tend to them daily to make sure they are growing strong and healthy. Whether you just keep them as pets or plan on using the fish for food, make sure you feed them appropriately and keep their tank or basin clean of any mold or algae that may start to crop up. The fish are going to be feeding your plants, so regardless of if you plan on using them for food or not, make sure they are healthy and have good living conditions. We suggest using freshwater fish such as tilapia or barramundi in your aquaponics system, as they grow fast and can tolerate diverse conditions. Other good options include trout in lower water temperatures, and you can even add other aquatic life such as snails and shrimp to your system.

Aquaponics may be a little more complicated, but once the setup is complete, most of the hard work is as well. Taking care of your vegetables will require the same efforts as any other hydroponics system and even less than a regular gardening method. Taking care of the marine life generally just means paying extra attention and spending extra time to make sure their water is clean and fresh, and that they are well-fed, healthy, and not over or underpopulating the tank. With the huge variety of benefits, there is no reason not to try your hand at this great method to improve your homestead!

Chapter 4:

Preserving Everything

Now that you know the basics of growing your own crops, it's time to learn about preserving and storing them. It's one thing to have all this homegrown food, but if you don't know proper preservation techniques, it can go bad quickly and all your hard work will be for naught. Homesteading encompasses more than just growing your own food; it is a lifestyle. Homesteading means tending to the land, taking care of it, and preserving what you take from it and giving back in order to live in harmony with the earth. Once you understand the art of growing, preserving, storing, and eventually, eating, you can extrapolate these ideals to the rest of your life, and that is when you will truly be a homesteader.

There are many ways in which you can preserve both the crops you grow and the meat from animals you raise, as well as ways to use every part of the plant or animal, to ensure almost nothing goes to waste. Done properly, homesteading can have little to no negative environmental impact, and you can save and store your homegrown goods to last you as long as you need. Preserving your food is especially important for the wintertime when you may be unable to grow crops, meaning you'll need to store up as much as you can during the summer if you want to survive out on your own.

Canning Food

If done properly, canning food is a safe and effective method at storing your goods and keeping them fresh for longer. The process involves placing food in jars and sealing them so that no microorganisms or bacteria can get in and cause the food to spoil. Canning can also deactivate enzymes in the food that cause it to spoil when left out in the open for long periods of time. This allows you to keep food fresh for as long as you may need, and when it comes time to use, you can simply open a jar.

If your canning process is not done properly, it can cause the food to rot, or worse, have dangerous health effects. Microorganisms that you are unable to see can grow inside your canned food without your knowledge, and some of them are harmful to humans when consumed. One example is the *Clostridium botulinum* bacteria, which can grow and release spores in your food. This bacteria is the cause of botulism, and if the spores are left to grow, then they can produce a deadly botulinum toxin. It is very important when canning your food to ensure that you have thoroughly researched the best method to can that specific item.

So, what are some canning methods? Let's go over a few. In general, there are three main ways to safely can your goods: a boiling water bath method, an atmospheric steam canning method, and the pressure canning method. Which method you use will vary depending on what you are trying to preserve, but you should always be following one of these methods.

Boiling Water Bath Method

This method of canning is best for fruits, jams, and jellies, as well as tomatoes and pickles. The process involves jarring and sealing your foods, then dipping the jars into a pot of water and bringing it to a boil. You want to be sure that the jar is completely submerged during this process, so that every inch is heated correctly. By bringing the water to a boil, you will kill any bacteria or spores that may have been growing on your food, as they cannot survive at high temperatures.

For this method to work correctly, you must be sure that the water level is at approximately one inch above the lid of the jar. Once the water comes to a boil, keep it heated for at least 10 minutes or whatever the recommended processing time is for the food you are preserving. Once the processing time has passed, turn off the heat and let the jars sit in the water for five minutes or longer before you go to remove them. Carefully place the jars on a cooling rack and leave them there for 12-24 hours. Don't touch or try to adjust the lid or any part of the jar until they have completely cooled. Once the jars have cooled, you can check that they are properly sealed. If they are, then you can proceed to storing them. If you find that the jar is not sealed properly, do not try to adjust the lid, as breaking the seal cannot be undone. Instead, take the jar, and place it in the fridge to consume within a few days.

This method works great for high-acid foods with a pH balance below 4.6 with no extra work needed. Foods such as fruits and properly pickled vegetables fall into this category. For low-acid foods such as tomatoes and figs which have a pH value closer to 4.6, an acidic solution must be added to ensure that the bacteria will be completely killed off. Add a few spoons of lemon juice or citric acid to your jar to ensure that all the spores are killed, and your food is safely preserved.

Atmospheric Steam Canning Method

The second method of canning is good for naturally acidic or properly acidified foods such as fruits, preservatives, and pickled vegetables. This method should not be used for low-acid foods such as vegetables or meat. The reason being similar to that of the previous method: you want to ensure that any bacteria or spores that may be within the jar are properly neutralized and killed. With a steam canner, you cannot add acidic liquid to the steam, so only use this method for foods that are high-acid.

The steam canner works similarly to the boiling bath method. The jars are placed on a rack above a reservoir of water, and the steam created from the boiling water provides a thermal treatment for the jars. This method uses less water and can be a lot faster than the boiling bath method. The steam canner also requires less energy and time to reach its peak point, at which the jars are safely preserved.

For this method to work best, preheat the jars before you put them into the steam canner, and try to minimize cooling before the process can occur. Once the jars are in the steam canner properly, allow the full processing time to pass. Once they have been properly processed, turn off the heat and carefully remove the lid of the steam canner. Do not touch the jars for at least five minutes while they cool off a bit. Afterwards, move the jars to a cooling rack, just as in the previous method, and allow them to sit for 12-24 hours before checking that they've been properly sealed.

Pressure Canning Method

The third and final canning method is pressure canning. This is the only method that is safe and functional for low-acid foods such as vegetables, meat, poultry, and seafood. Due to the dangers of botulism and these bacteria, these foods must be canned using a pressure canner. The jars of food you want to preserve must be placed in a couple inches of water and boiled to at least 240°F. This level of heat can only be reached by a pressure canner.

To use the pressure canner, prep your jars and place them into the canner with two to three inches of water surrounding the bottom. The water should be hot but not yet boiling. Once the jars are all properly placed, shut the lid to the canner and make sure the steam cannot escape except through the vent. Turn heat on high, and once the steam begins to escape through the vent of the pressure canner, let it escape steadily for 10 or so minutes. After that, close the vent to create the pressure within the canner. Some pressure canners will allow you to control the amount of pressure placed and some you will have to monitor yourself. Allow the pressure to rise to the correct amount as recommended, and then turn the heat down slightly to maintain that level. Once the weight on the pressure canner begins to move slightly, begin counting the processing time. Once the processing time has elapsed, turn off the heat and remove the canner if you can. It will take about a half an hour for the pressure to return to zero, and once it has, you can remove the lid facing away from you so that the steam doesn't burn you when it escapes. Then, you can place your jars on a cooling rack and follow the same steps as with the other methods for storage.

Preparing to Can

When you prepare to can your food, always gather your equipment first, get set up, and grab the food last. This ensures that the food is only sitting out for the shortest amount of time possible. Also, try to follow these preservation methods only on foods that are properly ripened and not overly ripe. You also don't want to overdo it. Only gather as much as you will be able to handle in two or three hours. If you gather too much food and have it sitting out for too long while you are working, some of it will slowly start to go bad before you can even get it in the containers.

When you gather your jars and lids, inspect them individually to ensure that there are no cracks or breaks and that all of them seal properly. Wash them thoroughly, and try to keep them warm. Keeping the jars warm when you add the food will prevent any breaks during the canning process. You should also be sure to use two-piece lids as they are safest and work best.

There are a couple different ways to pack your jars. First is raw packing. This is where you put the food directly into the jar without any other prep. For this method, be sure to pack foods into the jar as tightly as you can, as most foods will shrink during the process. The exception is for corn, beans, potatoes, and peas, as they actually expand during canning. After you've packed the food into the jar, add boiling water, juice, or warmed syrup over the food until it is all completely covered. Anywhere between a half a cup to 1½ cups of water should be good for a quart jar.

The second method is to hot-pack your jars. This simply means that you heat your food first by either boiling it or cooking it before adding it to the jars with the boiling liquid. In this process, the food will have already undergone the shrinkage from the heat, so you can pack the jars just loosely enough to allow the liquid to fully submerge the food inside. Then, same as before, seal your jar with the lid and make sure it is nice and tight.

When adding your food to the jars, keep the area and jars as clean as possible. Then, you can add your jars to the water or steam canner and begin boiling. Make sure to leave the jars in the boiling water or steam canner for at least 10 minutes. This is to ensure that they are properly sterilized during the process. Then, remove the jars carefully and try not to burn yourself, and it's on to storage.

Most two-piece jars will make a 'pop' noise when you tap on the lid if they are sealed properly. While the jars are cooling, this is your indicator on whether or not they have been properly sealed. If you don't hear the noise, refrigerate the jar and use the food within two to three days. Jars that are properly sealed can be stored for extended periods of time. When you put your jars in storage, try to organize them with the ones containing the least liquid at the front. These will be the ones you want to make a note to use first.

It is best to store your canned food in a clean, cool, dry, and dark place, such as a basement or cellar. Ideal temperature is between 50 and 70°F. Canned food left in the sun or in hot conditions will spoil faster; same with damp conditions where water may corrode the lids and cause rust. Once you have your jars in a dry, cool place, you can keep them stored for around a year. Depending on what you are storing, they may last longer or shorter, but generally, the rule of thumb is to use your stores by the one-year mark.

Drying Food

Another option for preserving your food is dehydration or drying it out. This simple method ensures that your food stays good for longer and can be extremely beneficial for life on the homestead. By dehydrating your food, you effectively remove any water from it and can prevent it from spoiling for pretty much forever. Drying food for preservation has actually been used by humans for thousands and thousands of years!

There are many advantages to preserving food through dehydration. Just like with canning, dried foods can be stored in a dark, cool place without any electricity or power necessary. Since they no longer have any water, most bacteria will die off immediately as they cannot generally survive without water. Drying foods also brings out new flavors that you may have never tried before. If you have ever eaten raisins, you know that they taste nothing like the grapes they once were.

There are a variety of different ways to dry food, and the method you choose will depend on what kind of food you are drying. One popular way is to use a smoker for meats and fish. If you have an oven that goes to a low enough temperature, you can even dry out your goods right on the top rack. The trick to drying out food, especially meats and fish, is that the temperature must be hot enough for the water to evaporate from the food, but not so much as to 'cook' the food. Cooking involves heating food to a degree in which the chemical composition of the food is changed in the process. This is what you DON'T want to happen in the dehydration practice!

Smoking meat can refer to two different things: preserving it or barbequing it. We will obviously be focusing on the preservation aspect of a smoker. Smoking meat is effectively cooking it at very low temperatures for an extended period of time in order to slowly dehydrate it without losing any of the delicious flavor and important nutrients. This method of food preservation has been used by humans for ages.

For most fruits and vegetables, you can just lay them out in the sun on a flat, dry surface to dry them out. Many herbs and some kinds of vegetables can simply be hung to dry. On hot sunny days, you can easily lay out a blanket or mat and dry out your fruits and veggies. You can also buy a special mat that enhances the process or make your own using aluminum foil. The foil catches the sunlight and reflects it, speeding up the drying process.

If you live in an area where hot, sunny days are not as reliable, you may want to invest in an electric dehydration machine or something similar. Excess humidity can also cause foods to mold quickly, so using an electric dehydrator is great for cloudy or rainy days. Regardless of how you dry your food, make sure you wash it thoroughly first so that it is nice and clean. You also may have to blanch your fruits and vegetables by dipping them in lemon juice or citric acid before dehydrating them in order to preserve their color and flavor. For most foods, you will need to cut everything into small, uniform pieces before using a dehydration machine. This goes for fruits, vegetables, and meats as well, and be sure to remove any fatty sections of the meat before drying it. Cutting your fruits and veggies into small pieces can also be useful for letting them dry in the sunlight, as the increased surface area can slightly speed up the process.

To store your dehydrated foods, first allow them to cool before packing them in airtight containers or plastic bags. Dried foods should always be stored in a cool, dry, dark place, just like canned foods. This is to optimize the preservation and avoid having the food spoil due to heat or water damage. Dehydrated food can generally last between six months to a year in storage.

The Art of Homesteading

Preserving is not just about food. To truly live a homestead lifestyle, the values of preservation and recycling must be transferred from simple food storage methods to an entire mindset and way of living. Once you start your homestead, you will begin to look at everything you own and wonder how it can be reused and upcycled. Our goal with teaching you to homestead is to change your way of thinking, so that you can see how to be more sustainable in every aspect of your life!

By the time you start working on your homestead, you should be looking to shift your mindset from the capitalist society to which you may be accustomed, to a sustainable, agrarian perspective on life. Think about what you need, not what you want. Consider the land your partner, not your property, and your homestead is not just a way to make food yourself, but a way to sustain you, your family, and even your community through sustainable practices. On the homestead, hard work, focus, and skill is what's going to keep you going, not money and materials. We want you to be able to shift your mindset more towards "make do or do without" and away from unsustainable, consumerist ideals that harm our planet.

Historically, homesteading was a way of living; and not just any way of living, but it was the *only* way. Now, over time and progress, we have all the resources we need available at our fingertips, and it has made us lazy and naive as a society. Homesteading connected us to the earth, to our food, and to our families and communities. The way we live now, in a society run by capitalism and consumerism, we are losing those connections, and what's worse, we are destroying the earth. We can still get back to the good life, though, through hard work, commitment, and determination. Homesteading can bring us back to what's important, and that in itself is art.

Building up your homestead can show others that this way of living is not only feasible, but highly successful and fulfilling. It may require more direct work to satisfy your needs, but it is so much more rewarding than anything else I have ever done. Through your homestead, you can create a community. Find others who have similar values to you, teach those around you about the joys of this life, and raise your locality up to the standards of preservation and sustainability we are trying to achieve.

When we talk about preservation, we don't just mean preserving food so that you have some saved for later. We are talking about the preservation and reuse of everything you have. Old tools can be taken apart and used to build something new, scraps and leftovers can be composted or fed to animals, and excess materials can be used for new projects or given to those in need. To truly be living the homestead lifestyle is to be 100 percent sustainable in your life so that you leave no garbage behind. It seems like a hard task at first, but once you start thinking of homesteading as a way of living, you will be able to accept that you can do anything.

Learn to apply these preservation skills and values to all aspects of your life. For example, preserve cheese by creating a wax seal around it, similar to canning your food. Try your hand at salt curing meats to help them last longer without using electricity or power. You can make homemade cheese in a DIY cheese press, homemade oils, vinegars, and more, and you can even learn to build an outdoor oven using stones and bricks or learn how to bake food without an oven at all. There are so many ways to constantly be improving, upgrading, and outdoing yourself and your homestead, and that's the beauty of it. You will never reach the perfect level or have the perfect homestead because there are always ways to do better!

Chapter 5:

Creating a Truly Optimized System

Now that your homestead is set up, and you've started growing and preserving, the next step is to optimize your homestead. Optimizing the processes on your homestead can take you to the next level, from growing your own food to becoming a truly sustainable homestead. You have only just started your journey to sustainable living, and in this next chapter, we are going to discuss all the ways you can integrate this new mindset into all aspects of your life.

Composting

We've discussed composting a few times already. However, it's time to go into some important details. Why should you compost? Well first of all, composting is just a way of recycling organic materials. Instead of putting scraps in the garbage and having them get sent off to a dump or landfill that will promote pollution, composting organic leftovers gives it new life. Organic materials such as food and yard waste can contribute to up to 50 percent of the average household trash. Reducing your waste by up to 50 percent is huge! Remember, homesteading is all about reusing materials and wasting as little as possible, and composting organic scraps is part of that outlook.

Composting can reduce your carbon footprint, and it can also benefit your homestead directly. When organic material breaks down, it becomes a great natural fertilizer for your garden. Adding compost to the soil where your crops grow promotes strong and healthy plant growth through a multitude of different functions.

Composting is a great way to take your homestead to the next level, and on top of that, it helps to reduce greenhouse gases on a larger scale as well. It can be hard to take a look at the bigger picture sometimes and step outside our small view of the world, but if we want to live sustainably and treat the earth right, we *must*. When you put out your trash bin at the corner on garbage day, you may not think about where that garbage goes: off to some dump somewhere. Not only do these huge dumps and landfills contribute to pollution, but the trucks that carry all the trash are also emitting carbon dioxide and other gases into the air, polluting our environment even further.

First of all, compost can increase the organic materials in your soil. This will make the soil more nutrient-dense and can help the plants better absorb these nutrients. Adding compost to your soil can also strengthen plant growth by keeping the soil pH levels balanced. Not only that, but adding compost to soil can also make clay-like soils more airy and easier to work with, while making sandier soils better equipped to retain water. Compost can even help regulate soil temperatures by insulating the soil around the plants. Using your compost as a natural fertilizer for your crops is especially good, because unlike store-bought fertilizers, compost will naturally regulate and release nutrients into the soil slowly and at a steady pace. It also won't harm any of your plants like some chemical fertilizers can.

One way to upgrade your compost game is to add worms into the mix. 'Vermicompost', as it's called when worms are introduced into the compost system, is especially good for homestead life, as it provides many more benefits. On top of all the already mentioned benefits of composting, vermicompost speeds up the process by which the organic materials are broken down and turned to fertilizer. Not only that, but the compost which the worms create can be used in a concentrated form as a natural weed killer, keeping your homestead clear of any invasive plants that could threaten to overrun your crops.

Making the Perfect Compost

Creating a great, natural compost right in your backyard is super simple. The only materials you will need beforehand are a large bin with a lid and some organic matter to get it started. A good compost is layered with a mix of brown and green organic materials and sits out on a flat surface that faces the sun. Heat from the sun can help your scraps decompose faster, so you won't have to wait as long before using it as fertilizer.

Once you've found a spot for your compost bin, start with a first layer of coarse, brown materials. Things like twigs and sticks; paper egg cartons if you have them. This bottom layer will help with water drainage and keep the bottom of your bin from getting moldy. The next layer should be dry and flat. We recommend you cover the surface of the coarse layer with dried leaves and newspaper. After that, alternate between brown layers, which are going to be carbon-based materials, and green layers of nitrogen-based materials. Some great brown compost materials include pine needles, dried leaves and sticks, dried grass clippings and yard waste, paper towels and napkins, bits of cardboard, shredded, brown paper bags, and more. For green compost materials, try using green leaves and garden waste, egg shells, scraps of fruits and vegetables, tea bags and coffee grounds, and even flowers.

Once you've set up the first few layers of your compost, you can leave it be. As you collect waste from your kitchen and yard, add it to your compost bin, making sure to add layers of brown as well. One great trick to remembering to toss your scraps in the compost is by keeping a smaller compost bin in your kitchen under the sink or in another place where the smell won't bother you or attract bugs. You can dump all your leftovers and scraps into the small bin or container, and once it fills up, transfer it to your compost bin. Keep adding to your compost bin until it is full.

As the compost decomposes, the materials in the bin will shrink. Make sure that when you are adding materials to the bin, you mix them in properly with the layers near the bottom so that it decomposes all evenly. Your compost should maintain a balanced level of moisture, meaning you may need to add some water if it is too dry or wring out materials that are waterlogged before mixing them into the heap. Be sure to mix or flip your compost every week or so to keep it even, help the process of breaking down the materials, and eliminate any odor.

You will know the compost is complete when it is dark and has a crumbly, earthy texture. It should look and smell similar to soil. Finished compost will usually have risen to the top of the bin, so you can easily remove it. Remove the finished compost, taking care to leave anything that has not finished in the bin to continue decomposing. Then, you can use the finished compost as fertilizer.

There are a few things you should be wary NOT to compost, as they could prevent the process or even harm your garden. Avoid adding any meats, oils, or grease to your compost bin, as they will not decompose along with the rest of the materials. Any weeds that you pull from your yard should also stay separated from your compost, as they generally reproduce by dropping seeds everywhere, and could start growing right in your compost bin. Obviously, any plant materials that are diseased or moldy should not be added to the compost, either, at the risk of ruining the entire bin, and any wood chips or sawdust from pressure-treated wood should be avoided as well. Dairy products are also a huge no-go for your compost, as they decompose differently from the rest of these materials, and they don't smell so great either.

Companion Planting

Companion planting is a great way to optimize your homestead and highly effective at promoting healthy crop growth. Companion planting is essentially just growing two or more species of crops next to or near each other in order for the plants to form a symbiotic relationship and benefit from each other's close presence. It may seem silly to say that plants can have best friends that make them better, but really, companion planting is just a gardening strategy that promotes growth by putting mutually beneficial plants near each other.

How does companion planting work, you wonder? Well, there are a variety of reasons two plants may benefit from being near each other. Growing a nitrogen-fixing plant next to a nonnitrogen-fixing plant can help balance soil fertility and promote growth for both plants. Large plants can often be used as natural trellises for smaller plants that require one. A tall plant can easily provide scaffolding for a smaller, climbing plant to grow upon. Large plants can also be used to regulate sunlight and heat for smaller plants that may thrive better in the shadow of their larger partner. A companion plant may even be able to keep away pests by masking their partner or confusing the pests that may be nearby. There are so many benefits to companion planting, and when done correctly, it can take your homestead to the next level.

The most well-known example of companion planting is the "Three Sister" trio of corn or maize, climbing beans, and winter squash. This trio was often grown together by Native American communities due to their complementary nature, and the practice has since been passed on to homesteaders and gardeners far and wide. The tall corn can support the climbing beans, and the winter squash protects the soil around the plants from too much moisture or heat. The big, prickly leaves of the squash also prevent pests from making their home in your plants and discourage weed growth as well. Climbing beans are also a nitrogen-fixing plant and pretty fast-growing, so they provide nitrogen for the corn and squash as all three grow together.

Obviously, corn and beans are a great pair as already mentioned, but there are so many other pairings and companion plants of which you can make use. Tomatoes and carrots, for example; the tomatoes provide shade and pest control while the carrots grow underground and aerate the soil. Planting chives near your lettuce and spinach can repel pests that are naturally attracted to leafy greens. Herbs are especially useful as companion plants, as many of them have properties that deter pests and discourage weed growth. Basil, parsley, and borage all pair well with tomatoes, as they repel or distract many pests from going near the tomatoes and attract bees to improve pollination. Another great companion plant for beans and cucumbers is sunflowers, as they grow tall and strong and can provide shade as they always face the sun.

Companion planting can be tricky at first, but once you get the hang of it, the benefits are innumerable. Once you find yourself getting into the rhythm of your homesteading life, try some of these combinations we mentioned and watch how your plants flourish. After a while, companion planting will become second nature to you, and you'll even be able to come up with your own combinations that you discover work well together.

Beehives

Beehives are another amazing way to increase productivity on your homestead and promote sustainability in congruity with Mother Nature. Bees are incredible animals that can improve your homestead exponentially. It takes just as much work to care for a beehive as it does to care for your veggies, possibly even less, and the bees will help your crops thrive. Plus, you can harvest honey from the bees regularly that you can then store or sell for some extra profit.

Before getting started with your bee colony, take into account a few different factors. First, research the laws and regulations surrounding beekeeping in your area. Certain regions have limits on how many colonies you can keep in a certain amount of space. Plus, if you are working with limited space, be sure to consult your family, neighbors, and anyone else who may be affected by your bees. You are going to need a place to keep them. Beyond just outside in your yard or garden, your bee colony should be kept off the ground so as to dissuade any wild animals from going near it. Keeping the boxes up above ground on a bench or a stand made of cement blocks works, although you may want something more permanent depending on the scope of your homestead.

To care for a bee colony on your homestead, there are a few things you will need. First, a bee box. You can purchase one from specialized garden centers and stores or online, or you can always make one yourself. If you are going to build your own bee box, make sure to do your research beforehand, as you want to build a space where the colony can survive and thrive. Bee boxes are relatively simple to build yourself, and the only materials you will need are some plywood, a few boards, some trim-head screws, and a sheet of aluminum flashing. You'll also need some sheets of beeswax to help get the colony started. Making your own beehive box is not a difficult project, but there are quite a few intricate steps that need to be followed, so make sure you are prepared for the commitment.

If you aren't looking to raise your own colony just yet, but still want to attract bees to your homestead for their pollinator powers, try building a DIY beehouse. A beehouse is a little different from a beehive or box in that it isn't made to house an entire colony, but rather individual bees as they come through. Your native species of cavity-resting bees will be encouraged to come to your homestead and pollinate, mate, and even reproduce if you have a beehouse on your property. A beehouse with a variety of little tunnels, chambers, nooks, and crannies is the perfect spot for bees to rest between pollination and even find a mate with which to reproduce.

Though bumblebees form colonies with a queen, many species of bees are actually solitary and live their life without a queen or colony. They nest in small cavities and do not produce honey, but still greatly contribute to the pollination of our gardens and farms. These bees include digger bees, miner bees, sweat bees, squash bees, and blueberry bees, which are all ground-nesters. There are also mason bees and leaf-cutter bees that nest in hollow tunnels in trees or dead wood. These bees will build nests, lay their eggs, and seal it off once they mate. If you can provide a spot for these bees to mate and lay their eggs with a beehouse, the baby bees will all grow up on your homestead, attracting more bees with which to mate and providing free pollination for your crops.

To make a beehouse, all you need is a large frame and material that will provide a variety of different sizes and depths of tunnels or compartments for the bees. For your frame, you can build one out of spare planks of wood or reuse an old crate. Pieces of tree bark and hollowed branches, wooden blocks that you've hollowed out with a drill, and even old paper towel rolls or toilet paper rolls can be used to create the tunnels where the bees will rest and nest. When you put your beehouse together, make sure that the tunnels and compartments vary in size, length, and width so that the bees can have their pick. You can use twigs and branches, dried leaves, pine cones, and string or twine to tie it all together and keep the structure sturdy.

Beehouse maintenance is very simple. First of all, you don't want to use any pressure-treated wood in the house, as it may not be good for the bees. Try not to introduce any chemicals that may be harmful. To keep the beehouse clean, make sure to replace the wooden tunnels or paper tubes every year or so.

The best way to attract native pollinators is to grow native species of plants. Do some research on your local area, and find out which flowers or other plants are bee-attractors. Many native bees are specialists and only go after specific plants, so research is key here. Another tip is to add a sandbox to your garden near the beehouse. This will give ground-nesting bees a place to store their food and other resources. You should also add a source of water for your bees. A small tray or even pet bowl will work; just add some rocks and pebbles for the bees to sit on while they hydrate. Most importantly, avoid the use of pesticides on your homestead at all costs. Find other ways to keep pests from rooting around your vegetables, as pesticides can be harmful to the good bugs as well.

Farm Animals

Keeping animals on your homestead can be a lot of hard work, but it is also a great way to keep up your sustainability goals and keep your homestead active. Many animals also naturally produce food sources, such as chickens with their eggs, and the meat from these farm animals can keep you going through the wintertime. Keeping animals on your homestead is a great way to increase productivity, improve your self-reliance, and earn some extra profit.

Chickens

Chickens are probably the easiest animals to keep on your homestead. They take up relatively little space, are cheap to feed (especially if you grow corn or plants with a lot of excess seeds), and they produce eggs! They are outdoor birds that historically lived in forests, jungles, and fields and can survive well in almost any weather. Most of the work it takes to raise chickens is really just common sense. You need to feed them, keep their coop clean, and make sure they have enough space to go about their business.

There are really just three essential steps for caring for chickens: housing and shelter, food and water, and space. General convention says that a chicken house needs about one square foot of floor area per chicken. We recommend you go a little bigger if you have the space, especially if you plan on raising more than four or five chickens. The more you have, the messier that house is going to get. Building your own chicken house and coop is relatively simple, as they don't need many complex structures; just a shelter with nesting boxes and enough space for the chickens to rest comfortably.

Chickens live healthier and longer when they have a clean, secure shelter. They also naturally seek out shelter and protection when the sun sets, so having a house for your chickens to nest in is a necessity. While there are other options, such as pet cages and even free-range living, having a chicken house with a run is generally the best option for homestead living. This will keep your chickens safe from predators, provide them with a shelter that you can easily access and clean, and give them enough space to roam around without losing track of them. Fencing off an area for your chicken coop is easy enough, and building a chicken house yourself is a cheaper alternative to buying; that is not as complex as many other homestead projects.

To build your chicken house, you're going to need to keep a couple of things in mind. First, as already mentioned, make sure you build big enough to comfortably house all your chickens. For beginners, keeping track of more than four or five chickens can quickly become a lot to handle, so a small house with just a few residents is probably your best bet. Most chicken houses are also raised above ground, either on stilts or on a deck. This keeps the house clean from the dirt and moisture of the ground that could get in and not only dirty the chicken house, but also compromise the structure if it becomes moldy. You also want to avoid any cold or damp conditions within the chicken house as the chickens won't like it and could even become sick.

Aside from building a simple shed-like structure to house your chickens, you will also need nest boxes within the house. This is where your chickens rest and lay their eggs. To build a nest box is quite simple, as they are essentially just small compartments where your hens will go when they lay their eggs. Take or build a small wooden box of about two square inches, with a seven or eight inch perch on which the hens can sit. Make sure your nesting boxes are easy to handle, as you will need to remove and replace them into the chicken house often. All you need to do is fill the boxes with a layer of hay or straw for cushioning, and you're done! The perches should be a little higher than the nest boxes to prevent the birds from sleeping in them. Keep the nest boxes in a darker corner of the chicken house for privacy, so the hens will not be disturbed while laying their eggs.

To feed your chickens, keep a feeder full and accessible at all times, as well as a bowl or feeder of clean, fresh water. The feeder and water don't have to be placed within the chicken house, as the bird will likely knock them over often or contaminate the food and water, which will require cleaning. One hen will eat approximately 150g to 180g of feed pellets a day, so use that as the basis to add the right amount of feed for the number of chickens you are raising. Only provide them with enough food for two or three days at a time so as not to overfeed them, and the pellets will get stale and moldy after a few days. You can give your chickens corn, seeds, and even some green vegetables such as cabbage or cauliflower leaves as a treat in the afternoons, but don't feed them too much of this option, as they are not healthy for the chickens in excess.

Goats

Goats are a great homestead animal as they are easier to care for than many others, can provide both dairy and meat, and take up less space, food, and water than a cow would. Raising homestead goats is a perfect way to become more connected with your food sources and with the earth. Goats can provide milk for dairy products and meat, as well as benefit your homestead by helping with the workload. For example, they can carry a pack full of tools or equipment you may need, can clear away brush, and can even have endearing personalities that make them enjoyable companions.

The main thing to be concerned about with goats is space. Raising any animal will take up a sizable amount of acreage on your homestead, so it's important to do your research before making any decisions. Luckily, goats come in many different breeds, and there are larger ones that are good for hard work, and smaller ones such as the Nigerian Dwarf goat, which could be raised in your backyard. Regardless of what breed of goat you go with, they all require the same (and relatively simple) housing and food.

For shelter, goats don't require anything too elaborate. As long as they have a space that is dry, well-ventilated, draft-free, and protects them from the elements, they will be happy as can be. Whether it be a traditional barn or a simple three sided-shelter, that depends on you and your homestead. Whatever works best and is most suited to the space you have will be fine, as long as you keep this in consideration before acquiring the goat. You'll also need good fencing around the area you plan on keeping your goat(s), to keep them from running wild around your homestead and keep predators away.

For food and water, goats don't require much. A simple five gallon bucket of clean water will suffice for their drinking source, and you will only have to change it out or refill it every day or two depending on how big or how many goats you have. Goats love to eat from a variety of different plants, bushes, and shrubs, though most homesteads are not equipped to provide goats with the space they need for browsing. Feed them from a trough or bucket with good quality, dry grass or hay. If it is time to milk a doe, you may want to supplement their food with alfalfa leaves or other grains such as corn, oats, and barley, to provide them with some extra protein, vitamins, and minerals. Many minerals, especially salt, are very important for goat health, so you may want to consider giving your goat a salt lick stone. This is up to your discretion.

Aside from breeding goats for their milk and meat, there are so many other benefits to having goats on your homestead. They can improve your pasture as they eat just about any kind of plant if you let them. Goats actually love poison ivy, so if you ever find yourself with a poison ivy problem, this could be an easy solution. They will also eat weeds and other shrubbery you may want to clear away. Goat droppings can also be used directly in your garden as fertilizer and don't need to be composted first. Goats are a herd animal and live better, longer lives when kept together, so take that into consideration as well before you decide if you want them on your farm. It is likely you won't be able to keep just one, but will have at least two or three of these beauties running around.

Pigs

Raising pigs can be so rewarding, as it is often a challenge, but they are such loving creatures you won't even realize that you're doing hard work when you are around them. There are also many benefits to having pigs on your homestead, as they can eliminate waste and provide you with much-needed, protein-dense meat. Owning pigs isn't for everyone, but if you find yourself up to the challenge of taking on another animal in your homestead, this is the one we recommend.

The easiest part of raising pigs on your homestead is that they will eat just about anything. Make sure they have a clean supply of water in their pen and a trough to fill with food, and that's pretty much all there is to worry about. Pigs will eat any leftover scraps from your kitchen, and they can even eat dairy products, meaning milk and cheese won't go to waste. Feeding your pigs expired products is fine, too; as long as they aren't moldy or clearly diseased, it should be completely safe and healthy for them. If you plan on selling the meat from your pigs for profit, make sure you boil any leftover food you do give them for at least 30 minutes to be extra sure that any microorganisms or bacteria living in the food that could be harmful have been killed.

The only downside to pigs eating just about anything is that they have to poop A LOT. Now, pigs are actually a lot smarter than we believe and a lot cleaner than we give them credit for, believe it or not. They will generally designate a specific corner or section of the pen to do their business, while keeping the rest of their area exceptionally clean. That being said, the one corner that isn't clean will be very smelly and require daily cleaning by you. As I said, pigs are smart, which means that they may try to escape their pen every once and a while. Make sure that the fencing you use for the pigpen is sturdy and reliable and the gate has a complex lock that needs fine motor skills to open. Otherwise, you may wake up to see your whole field eaten up over night!

Having pigs on your homestead can also be beneficial to other animals. Pigs can actually keep your other animals healthy as parasites from other animals are unable to survive in pigs. This can be said about many animals, if you raise more than one species. Because pigs have a very different internal system than horses, cows, goats, and other farm animals, they are dead ends for any parasites. This can be done by letting the animals roam around in the same areas at different times. Letting the pigs graze after the goats are herded back into their pen will allow the pigs to eat up all the eggs or larvae from the goat parasites. The parasites will be unable to survive in the pigs' system and thus die off.

Staying Grounded on the Homestead

Now that you've started optimizing your homestead and perfecting your life, what's next? Well, the truth is that it's the same as before. Continue to grow, to improve, to fail and succeed, and to try new things. Even if the farm is running smoothly, there are always ways to improve, and if you are focused solely on the physical aspects of your homestead and the outcomes of your work, then you aren't living a true homestead life. Without a calm and centered outlook, you won't be able to properly take care of your homestead, and without the mindset of sustainability and coexistence, you won't be able to live in harmony with your homestead.

The most important thing to remember when living on your homestead is to always remain grounded. Keeping your head clear and your mind focused is just as important to optimizing your homestead as adding compost or raising animals. Without the proper mindset, all you have is a bunch of tools and equipment and a big backyard. What does it mean to be 'grounded'? It means you are keeping yourself in the present, not worrying too much about the outcome, but focusing more on the process. Feel your purpose on the homestead, and trust yourself to stay on the right path.

Creating a space for mindfulness is so important when homesteading. You need to be able to adapt to changes around you and learn to take challenges as they come to you. Take breaks when you need to, and always take time to yourself and find pleasure in the simple things. Life can be hard sometimes, especially on a homestead when you feel like you are almost constantly working. Make sure you are taking time to practice mindfulness; remind yourself how lucky you are to be going through this experience, and be proud of yourself for every little victory.

Staying active is not difficult on the homestead, but make sure you are doing activities you enjoy for fun, not just working to tend to the homestead 24/7. Take breaks to read, write, sing, or do whatever it is you may find peaceful and relaxing. Remember that taking care of your mind is just as important as taking care of your body and your homestead. Always prioritize your mental and emotional well-being. If something seems too overwhelming, take a step back and reevaluate what it is you are doing and why. If you can't find a solution you like, it's okay to give up and try again another time. Your homestead can only thrive if you yourself are thriving as well.

Chapter 6:

Homesteading for Profit

Now that you are living the homestead lifestyle, how can you continue to maintain the things you love in life, strive for abundance, and profit from all your hard work? There are countless ways to profit off of your homestead, and you shouldn't feel limited just because you've shifted your mindset to a more sustainable way of life. You can live sustainably and still have everything you've ever wanted; it just takes some hard work, some smart moves, and belief in your dreams. Don't feel cornered by the homesteading ideals of "simple living"; you can be a homesteader and a successful business person at the same time!

From selling food from your garden, to sewing your own clothes and making artisanal breads and jams, there are countless ways to profit from all the work you do on your homestead. All you need is a little push to kick-start your homestead business and take you from hobbyist to professional homesteader. First and foremost, you're already saving money if you're a homesteader, and you're doing it while saving the environment, too. You're already in control of your life, and you have all the tools necessary to start turning a profit.

Saving Money

There are so many easy ways to save money on your homestead. Obviously, you are already growing your own crops, saving on food, and even raising animals to provide you with the essential protein your body needs. But how else can you save some cash while living your best homesteader life? Well, let's discuss some options! All you need to do is take that homesteading mindset you've been cultivating all this time and apply it to your finances. How can you reuse what you've already got to save money on buying new? How can you take the materials at your disposal and turn them into the things you need for survival?

First and foremost, always cook from scratch instead of choosing prepackaged. You're living on a homestead that should be full of the fruits of your labor—literally! Why eat out or have food delivered when you have farm fresh goods right outside your door? The money you save on buying food when you are a homesteader is going to be your No. 1, biggest source of savings. You may not even realize how much money is spent on groceries and eating at restaurants until you give up on it altogether. That money can go towards better tools and equipment, better food and shelter for your animals, fixing up your kitchen, or any other of the many homesteading projects I'm sure you're just itching to take on soon.

Another great money-saving tip for homesteaders is DIY: Do it yourself. Nowadays, there are tutorials for just about anything accessible with the press of a button on your computer. You can make your own soaps, cleaning products, and even clothing! I definitely recommend learning how to knit or sew or even purchasing a sewing machine. They can be a little pricey, but worth it 100 times over if you use it right. Learning to mend ripped clothes or fix broken tools can save you a ton of money and time. Instead of shopping new, upcycle the old; try taking an old pair of jeans that no longer fit and turning them into shorts. Old clothing that is really unwearable can even be cut into strips and used as cleaning rags around the homestead. Remember, it's all about applying the mindset of sustainability to everything around you.

Finally, connect to your environment a little more. Instead of paying for television, movies, and other forms of entertainment to keep you occupied, try finding things to do that don't cost any money. Explore a new part of the area that you've never seen before, go for a swim in a nearby lake or river, take your animals on a walk outside the homestead, etc. There is such a huge and amazing world out there; you don't need to be cooped up inside all day! Borrow books from friends, neighbors, or even the local library instead of buying, and that way, when you finish, you can return them and they won't take up space cluttering up your home. Most importantly, remember to keep an open mind and always have your eyes peeled for new opportunities. There are always ways to improve and always new and exciting things to see and do.

Making Money

There are a variety of different ways to profit off the work you do on your homestead. Though you will most likely not be able to majorly profit immediately, with a steady work pace and consistent drive, you will break even and start earning an income in no time. A lot of the ways people make money on their homestead revolve around selling their goods. This means some extra work for preparing and packaging your foods or homemade goods, but you can sell at whatever price you set, as you will effectively be your own boss. Do some research, especially if you live nearby other homesteads or self-run businesses, and find out what's available in the market already and what there may be a greater need for in the future.

The best way to earn a profit from selling homemade or homegrown goods is to be consistent, reliable, and friendly. Making a name for yourself within your community can take some time, but don't give up. Get the word out and let people know what you have and how it can benefit them! You can even tell people that by buying from you, they are saving the planet by funding an eco-friendly business and a local food source.

As for what kinds of goods to sell, that's up to you. Of course, you can take your fresh produce directly to a farmers market, but you can also turn your crops into artisanal goods that will fetch a higher price. Selling homemade preserves like jam and honey, dried fruits or smoked meats, homemade cheese, herbs and spice mixes, and even homemade soaps and other cosmetics can all be very profitable if you know how to make them!

Homemade Jam

Making your own jam is relatively easy, especially once you are used to all the hard work that comes with life on the homestead. Homemade jam crafted with organic fruits from your homestead can be a great way to start making money, as so many people love jam, and you can make all kinds of different flavors depending on what you've got at your disposal. Turning your fruits into jam also preserves them longer, so any ripe berries you may have that are about to go bad can easily be cooked up into a delicious jam that lasts. This way, you can store it longer for your own pantry, or sell to your friends, family, and local community.

Jam is super easy to make and only has a few simple steps. All you need is the fruit of your choice, some granulated sugar, and an acid juice of your choice. As a general rule, I like to use about ¼ to ⅔ of a cup of sugar for every pound of fruit. This comes out to about 52 to 130 grams of sugar for 450 grams of fruit. Now, depending on what fruit you are using, you may need to include a couple extra steps. If your fruit has a peel or skin, make sure to remove that as well as any pits. This step is necessary for fruits like peaches and plums. For the acid juice, you can use a freshly squeezed lemon or even lime, some white vinegar, or any other acidic juice of your choice. This is necessary to activate the fruits naturally occurring pectin, which is what makes jam thick and gel-like.

First, cut up your fruit into small pieces. They don't need to be exact as it will all be cooked together later. In a bowl, mix the sugar with your fruit, and stir it around with your hands to ensure that all the fruit pieces are fully and evenly covered. If you are a beginner, start by adding only a quarter cup of sugar. Afterwards, you can taste a piece of fruit and decide whether you want your jam sweeter or not. Once this is done, cover the bowl, and let it sit in the fridge for 24 hours. This step allows the fruit to break down properly and can help remove liquid which will better dissolve the sugar. After the fruit has macerated in the fridge for a day, transfer it into an appropriately-sized pot and bring to a boil on high heat. Once the mixture is boiling, add a couple teaspoons of your acid juice. I highly recommend using lemon juice for this step as it is organic and can possibly even be found on your own homestead. Reduce the heat to medium-low, and stir often to make sure the jam is even. At this point, you can add any herbs or aromatics you may want for some extra flavor, or use a potato masher to smooth out any chunks if you are going for a smooth-textured jam.

To check if your jam is finished cooking, you can do a "plate test". Spoon a small amount of the jam from the pot onto a plate. If the jam is still runny, it needs to cook for longer. Once the jam holds its blob form on the plate, that's how you will know it is done cooking. From here, you can transfer your jam into jars, let it cool, and then keep in the refrigerator for up to a month. If your goal is to sell your jam, you may want to consider using a canning technique to seal the jars so that they last longer for your customers.

When it comes to jam-making, a lot of the work is based on preference. If you want a smoother or chunkier jam, you can cut different-sized chunks of fruit and mash it up while simmering. You can also add multiple fruits if you want to make a mixed jam, though don't go overboard or you'll muddle the flavors. One trick I like to do when making my own jam is to strain it once it's finished cooking and before putting it in the jar. For berry jam, especially blackberry or raspberry, straining it will help remove any small seeds that I, personally, don't like to eat.

Again, it is a preference thing and totally up to you and what kind of jam you want to make.

Dried Fruits

You already know how to dehydrate your fruits to make fruit leather; now it's time to package and sell! Dried fruits are especially good on-the-go snacks that can provide you with a delicious boost of energy while you are working, exercising, or just out and about. The trick to selling some good dried fruit—or really *any* product from your homestead—is good marketing and proper packaging. If you are homesteading in a rural area, it is more than likely that other homesteaders nearby will be doing *exactly* what you are doing, and trying to sell their goods. You need to make sure your product stands out, and let the people know exactly what they are supporting when they buy from you.

Dried fruit is durable and amenable, meaning pretty much any packaging will work as long as it is kept clean. You can use plastic bags or glass jars to wrap your dried fruits, and sell them individually or as a jumbled mix of all different flavors. When you sell your fruit, make sure to let customers know that they are making a difference by supporting you and your homestead, and be sure to tell them what goes into making these delicious goods. Giving customers some background information will help them feel more at ease purchasing from you, especially if they are a new customer. Sharing your stories may also influence them to try their hand at living more sustainably and may even persuade them to try homesteading.

Something as simple as dried fruits can have a huge impact on your community and the planet.

One great way to get the word out about your homemade goods is to start a website. Building a website is super easy and cheap, and there are plenty of options available to help you find the perfect format and style for your site. Having an online shop where people can make purchases and have the goods shipped to them is a great way to expand your market outside of your local community. Make sure to put up some information about yourself and your homestead, as well as each product you want to sell. You should also always add clear, high quality photos of your products, so that people can see what it is they will be receiving when they make their purchase.

Selling Meats

The first thing you need to know about selling meat from your homestead is the laws and regulations that must be followed. In the United States, the only legal way to sell meat that has been homegrown on your homestead is to have it slaughtered and butchered at a USDA (United States Department of Agriculture) inspected processing facility. Livestock must be harvested and butchered onsite in order to be lawfully sold to a retailer, at a farmers market, to restaurants, etc. This is called a "retailer's cut". The advantages to this are that you can sell the meat individually packaged as opposed to selling the entire animal and make a premium, maximizing the profit you can make from your meat.

The only problem with going this route is that the processing fees from the facility can be hefty. On top of that, USDA inspectors are few and far between, meaning that you may have to drive a far distance just to get your meat processed properly. This can seriously raise the costs and dissuade many homesteaders from going this route, as it may not be worth your while depending on how much meat you plan on selling. That's where the second option comes in, of course.

"Custom Butchery Exemption" is a way in which you can avoid going to a USDA-inspected facility; however, it is a little more complex and takes some extra work on your part. The details of this process are that you effectively sell the meat by selling the live animal wholesale and then make custom arrangements on behalf of the customer to get it custom butchered. "Custom meat" can include cattle, swine, sheep, or goat and does not need to be USDA-inspected when it is butchered. Custom meat is also legally only allowed to be used within the household by the owner. Thus, in order to follow the proper regulations, you need to make sure that your transaction is done for the *live animal*, not the meat itself. The transaction must be completed and ownership passed on to the customer, *prior* to the slaughter and butchery of the animal. Once the transaction is complete, you as the homesteader can have the butchering done on the customer's behalf.

Uninspected meat cannot be sold under any circumstances, so the butcher must mark the meat with a "Do Not Sell" label. This means that you limit your selling options, and the buyer of the animal must purchase and use all the meat themselves. Luckily, there are rules that allow for animals to be purchased by multiple buyers altogether. This means that cattle or larger animals can be divided into two or four pieces and sold to multiple consenting buyers. This method has advantages and disadvantages. As mentioned previously, you as the farmer will have to sell the meat in bulk, meaning the market for your product will be a lot smaller, and it may be hard to come by customers. The advantages are that you won't need to use a USDA-approved facility, meaning processing fees will certainly be a lot cheaper. Beyond that, the process will be less stressful for the animals as they won't have to endure the wait time and harsh conditions of a USDA-approved facility.

Selling meat can be tricky due to all the rules and regulations, so be careful and always do your research beforehand. Make sure you are fully aware of all the laws surrounding the selling and purchasing of live animals or butchered meat before making any commitments to customers, and if you are unsure about anything, it is always helpful to inquire with an inspector or official. You want your homestead to be successful, but not at the cost of breaking any food safety laws. These laws are in place for a reason; that mainly being the safety concerns surrounding food, particularly meats, and their preparation. If any of the processes between raising your animal to cooking your dinner are done incorrectly, or without proper health and safety measures, the food could be contaminated or unsafe for consumption. Always make sure you trust your butcher and anyone else who will be handling your livestock the same way you trust your waiter with your meal at a restaurant.

Herb and Spice Mixes

Creating your own mix of herbs or spice blends is super easy and fun! A lot of blends from the grocery store contain additives like MSG, so making homemade is actually healthier and can earn you a little income. All you need is the herbs and spices on your homestead, some small jars, and a little creativity. If you are going to sell individual spices, all you need is to package them up and add some labels. If you want to get a little fancy, though, making your own custom spice blends can be a great way to find a signature style for your homestead.

There are so many recipes available online for all different kinds of spice blends. Try to come up with some ideas based on what flavor profiles you like best, and then, experiment in your own kitchen to figure out what works well together. Obviously, you can go for some classics like an Italian or Mediterranean blend, but you can also make up your own combinations. Test out your spice combos at home with your family and even with your friends and peers. Once your test market—aka your friends—approve, get to bottling and selling!

One thing to remember with spice mixes is that people will probably want to try them out before purchasing, especially if you sell in a larger container. If you are selling at a farmers market or local shop, see if you can set up a sample tray. Add a little bit of spice mix to a small bowl with some olive oil and mix it up to create a dip, then allow people to try it out with pieces of bread or crackers. This will give them a good idea of the flavors without you having to cook up a bunch of homemade meals using all your spices.

Chicken Eggs

Selling your chicken eggs can be a great way to supplement your income and cover the cost of feed for your birds. Make sure to check the local laws and regulations regarding the sale of chicken eggs before you get started. You're also going to want to carefully clean the eggs before you sell them, as you and your family may not worry about some dirt on the shell, but customers might have a different opinion. The best way to keep your eggs clean is to keep the nesting boxes clean, so be sure to keep up with maintenance for your chickens each and every day.

Egg-sizing varies in some regions, but the general rule is that the size label increases every 0.25 ounces, starting at 1.25 oz for a peewee egg, 1.5 oz for a small, and going all the way to 2.5 oz for a jumbo. Now, proper sizing only has to be done for eggs that are going to be sold commercially, meaning to another vendor. If you just want to sell your eggs yourself with a stand or at a farmers market, you don't need to worry so much about the size. You can purchase plain egg cartons from a garden center or craft store, as you legally can't sell eggs in name brand cartons due to rules and rights surrounding branding. Make sure that when you sell your eggs you have a best before date on the carton as well!

One great tip for selling your homestead eggs is to raise chickens that lay different-colored eggs! Having a pop of color in those cartons can be very eye-catching and even exciting to buyers who generally shop at the grocery store and may only be used to white and brown eggs. You should also always give your customer details on how your chickens are raised. People will often be willing to spend a little more money on their food if they know it has been made sustainably and that the animals are happy and well cared for, of course.

Harvesting Honey and Beeswax

If you've decided to house a bee colony on your homestead, selling the honey and beeswax can fetch you a pretty penny. Beeswax has so many purposes; it's great for candles, polishing wood or leather, cosmetic use, arts and crafts, and so much more! Not to mention that fresh, locally-sourced honey is very on trend these days.

Beeswax can be sold both locally and commercially to individuals in the community and businesses alike. Many businesses use beeswax to make other products and having a good supplier is always necessary. If your apiary is large enough, you can definitely find some larger corporations that look for wholesale suppliers like you! Selling at local fairs, farmers markets, and even just from your own porch is another way to earn some income and grow your customer base. Whether you sell the beeswax in sheets or in the form of some other craft you've created, people will love these homestead goods.

Honey is great for local consumers, farmers markets, and even local restaurants or grocery stores. Many smaller businesses may be seeking to find locally-sourced ingredients for their own business recipes, and that's where you come into the picture. Providing a local cafe with fresh honey for their pastries and coffees can be a sweet deal (no pun intended) and gain you a reputation as a notable seller in your community.

Soapmaking and Cosmetics

Natural, homemade soap is another great way to earn an income on your homestead. Making your own soap is also relatively simple and can be done right from your kitchen. All you need to make homemade soap is lye, water, solid oils, liquid oils, and your scents. The scents can come from essential oils or any aromatics you may have growing on your homestead. You can also choose to add color to your soaps as well as extra decor like pressed flowers or seeds within the mix. There are plenty of recipes for easy homemade soaps available online, and most of them are super simple and easy to follow.

The simplest of soap recipes contain only six ingredients; 16 ounces of coconut oil, 14 ounces of palm oil, 21 ounces of olive oil, 19 ounces of distilled water, a two pound container of lye, and seven or so teaspoons of the essential oil of your choice (or any other ingredient you want to use for scent). This amount will provide you with enough for four full batches of soap. The first step is to put on some rubber gloves because handling lye can be harmful to your skin before it is properly mixed. Carefully measure 200 grams of lye and 19 ounces of distilled water, and then, mix the two together in a glass pitcher, stirring just long enough for all the lye to dissolve. The chemical reaction that ensues will cause the solution to heat up and release fumes; this is totally normal. Let the solution cool for about an hour before you continue.

Next step is to prepare your mold and measure out your fragrance. You can use one scent or combine multiple in different amounts, as long as you make sure that you are measuring out seven teaspoons of essential oils. Then, you are going to melt and mix all the oils, including the coconut, palm, and olive oils. Since some of these are solid at room temperature, you will need to melt them down before adding them. Once your lye mixture and your oils all reach the same temperature range of about 80 to 100°F, blend them together in a large pot. Always add the lye mixture to the oils and not the other way around. The mixture should turn cloudy, and continue to blend for about three or four minutes. You are aiming for the consistency of a runny pudding or melted jello, and once you reach this consistency, slowly and evenly mix in your fragrance or essential oils.

After that, all that's left is to pour the mixture carefully into your molds. Then, let it cool in the fridge or outside for at least 24 hours before removing it. Your soap can then be removed and cut into sizes of your preference. When cleaning up, make sure you scrub everything down properly. I recommend that you don't use any of the tools that interacted with the lye for any other purpose, as trace amounts may remain even after thorough cleaning.

Worms

One thing you may not have thought of when coming up with profitable homestead projects is raising and selling worms! As you know, worms are great for soil composition, compost, and so much more. They are an essential part of agriculture and homestead living. So, why not take this essential part of your life and make some money off of it?

Worms reproduce extremely rapidly and have so many benefits. Soil improvement, compost production, and even fishing! There are always people looking to buy worms, which seems silly because they live in the ground just about everywhere. Depending on how large you want to grow your worm business and how much space you have on your homestead, you're going to want to take a relatively large bin and fill it with soil. Next, make sure you have lots and lots of feedstock for your worms. This could be anything from animal manure to dried leaves and plants to shredded newspapers. Worms love to eat all kinds of organic materials. Once you introduce the worms to the bin, make sure to keep the environment comfortable for them. Worms thrive in warm, moist places, so keep your soil in a dark and warm place, adding water as often as necessary.

When worms breed, they secrete a cocoon that can contain any number of eggs between one and about 20, depending on the species. Over the spring, worms may continue to mate every three or four days throughout the entire season, producing so many baby worms that you won't know what to do with them! Once they hatch, you can gather up your worms and package them in small containers with enough nutrient-dense soil to keep them happy and fat when you sell. Worms are generally sold at a price by the pound, so find a container to package them with this in mind.

You can then sell your worms commercially to large agriculture corporations that may be in need or locally to farmers and fishers in your community. My own father loves fishing, and when I was young, I used to always beg him to buy me an extra bucket of worms so that I could raise a little worm family in the backyard. Maybe it was an early sign that I would be a homesteader, or maybe I was just a silly child. Either way, I never got my worms until I grew up and started raising them myself.

Host Events

One last idea for making a profit on your homestead is to host events! Homesteads and farms can be great venues for parties and celebrations such as weddings, community events, and even educational trips for businesses and schools. Your homestead can be a great scenic location for important moments in other people's lives.

Hosting celebrations like weddings can be a great way to supplement your income if you've got the space and supplies. Plus, your duties as the venue are relatively simple. You can hire people to set up beforehand and clean up afterwards or negotiate a contract in which that is the guest's responsibility. Either way, people will pay a lot to have their wedding or other celebration in the perfect spot, and a homestead is the perfect combination of rustic, outdoorsy, and scenic! Especially if you are growing colorful plants and flowers that act as built-in decor, hosting parties and events on your property can be a great way to make some money and introduce new people to homesteading and any other products you may be selling.

Hosting academic events like a school field trip can also be a great way to teach children about the joys and hardships of homesteading. Schools are always looking for new ways to get kids interested in learning and keep them entertained. Your homestead is the perfect location for them to learn all about homegrown food, hard work ethic, and sustainable living. You can help kids grow up to be passionate, empowered, eco-warriors who may even start their own homesteads one day; all of this, while also getting paid for hosting!

Running activities and events for community members or even corporate retreats is another great idea. Hard work on a farm is exactly what so many businesses are in need of when they are searching for team-building exercises that can increase company morale and build strong work ethic. Plus, living on a beautiful homestead for a night or two is a perfect little mini vacation for most city people, even if they do have to work all day.

Talk to your local community event organizers, such as public officials and community center staff, to find out more about how your homestead can be used for public events and activities. Even a small homestead can be useful for community-run events like outdoor movie nights, cooking classes, and so much more. Plus, this is a great way to become closer to your neighbors and peers. You can make friends, get more people interested in the homestead lifestyle, and even grow your customer base for many of your products. Additionally, for any of these events, you can always have a little stand set up with other goods you are selling like your jams or chicken eggs. That way, not only will you profit from hosting the events, but you can also earn a nice bonus from visitors who want to bring home a souvenir.

Conclusion

Congratulations! You've made it to the end of the guide, and you've successfully educated yourself on all the basics of a good homestead. What comes next is up to you. Do you want to start raising chickens in your backyard? Or maybe you are going to start a little vegetable garden? Maybe, you even feel confident enough to start running a full homestead, top to bottom? Whatever your decision, we at Small Footprint Press are proud of you for making it this far and learning all the tricks to sustainable homestead living.

We hope that this guidebook helped you to not only learn the basics of how to live on a homestead, but also taught you the importance of why you *should*. We are all responsible for the well-being of this planet, and living in a capitalist, consumption-based society is simply not sustainable anymore; in fact, it never *was*. We need to collectively shift away from a consumer mindset and become producers of our own needs and wants if we are going to truly make progress towards taking better care of the earth. It is your responsibility, just as much as the next person, to ensure a happy, healthy, and safe place from which future generations can benefit. Living the homesteader lifestyle is just the beginning.

You've learned how to prepare yourself mentally and physically for homesteading. You've learned about growing crops and raising animals. You've also learned about making things from scratch, building shelters and sheds, preserving food and materials for later use, and even how to expand your wealth and share with your community. Now it is time for you to take this knowledge and put it to good use. All this reading will have been for nothing if you don't go out and start living more sustainably today.

If you take even just one lesson away from this, let it be that your mindset is the most important tool at your disposal. You truly can do anything you put your mind to so long as you believe in yourself, work hard, and never give up. It may sound cheesy, but it is nothing but the truth. Just go online and look up how many successful homesteaders are sharing their stories. It is possible to live sustainably, to grow and serve your own food, and to prepare for the worst and expect the best. Everything we've talked about throughout this entire book is possible for you, as long as you put your mind to it.

Shifting your mindset can be hard work, but it is absolutely crucial, especially in this day and age. If we want to leave this world a better place than we found it, we must all do our share to restore and revive Mother Nature through sustainable, agricultural practices, proper recycling and reusing of materials and resources, and actively working towards 100 percent sustainability. You may not be able to get there right away—in fact, it would be impossible to try—but we can all get there eventually. Homesteading wherever you live is possible!

When it comes to homesteading, or even just simple gardening, the work you put in is what you will see in return. The more work you put into your homestead, the better it will be and the better you will feel. It is a difficult task, yes, and it takes a lot of energy, effort, and commitment, but done properly, it is so worth it. Your homegrown food will taste a million times better even just knowing that you made it completely yourself and in an environmentally-conscious fashion. Plus, the satisfaction and fulfillment you will feel when you finally eat that first bite; that alone is worth all the fast food in the world!

There you have it—all the knowledge you need to start your homestead, right in your very own backyard. Now that you've finished reading and researching, it's time to get to work. Whether it be on a huge plot of farmland, in your suburban backyard, or even just on your front porch, you can start living the homesteader life today!

References

5 steps to homestead success and a winning mindset. (2012, November 28). Joybilee® Farm | DIY | Herbs | Gardening |. https://joybileefarm.com/5-steps-to-homestead-abundance/

7 Easy Steps to Composting | City of Leduc. (2019). Leduc.ca. https://www.leduc.ca/composting/7-easy-steps-composting

7 Tips to Help You Sell Your Farm Fresh Eggs For More Money. (n.d.). Fresh Eggs Daily®. https://www.fresheggsdaily.blog/2017/05/7-tips-to-help-you-sell-your-farm-fresh.html

8 Ways to Build a More Sustainable Homestead. (2020, June 28). Kaits Garden. https://kaitsgarden.com/2020/06/27/8-ways-to-build-a-more-sustainable-homestead/

9 Ways to Stay Grounded in Uncertain Times | Coping With COVID-19 | Stamford Health. (n.d.). **Www.stamfordhealth.org**. https://www.stamfordhealth.org/healthflash-blog/infectious-disease/9-ways-to-stay-grounded/

11 Ways to Stick to Your Budget. (n.d.). **Www.valleyfirst.com**. https://www.valleyfirst.com/simple-advice/money-advice/ways-to-stick-to-your-budget

admin, & admin. (2019, July 27). *A Complete Guide to Solar Electric Fences: Build an Off-Grid Fence.* Greencoast.org. https://greencoast.org/solar-electric-fence/

Avery, J. (2018, January 8). *How To Stay Committed To Reaching Your Goals.* Farm Homestead. https://farmhomestead.com/how-to-stay-committed-to-reaching-your-goals/

Basic Chicken Keeping Hints & Tips | Chicken Houses & Coops | Poultry Supplies. (n.d.). **Www.flytesofancy.co.uk**. https://www.flytesofancy.co.uk/chickenhouses/basic_chicken_keeping.html

Benefits of Composting. (n.d.). Less Is More. https://lessismore.org/materials/72-benefits-of-composting/

Careta, M. (2015, June 8). *The 5 Most Important Crops You Need For Survival.* Off the Grid News. https://www.offthegridnews.com/survival-gardening-2/the-5-most-important-crops-you-need-for-survival/

Carleo, J. (2017, January). *FS1263: Ultra-Niche Crop Series: Writing SMART Goals for Your Farm (Rutgers NJAES).* Njaes.rutgers.edu. https://njaes.rutgers.edu/fs1263/

Charbonneau, J. (2017, February 3). *33 Homestead Plants that are Easy to Grow.* Survival Sullivan. https://www.survivalsullivan.com/33-easy-grow-plants-homestead-prepper/

Doval, C. (2018, December 11). *What is Sustainable Agriculture?* Sustainable Agriculture Research & Education Program. https://sarep.ucdavis.edu/sustainable-ag

familydoctor.org editorial staff. (2010, May). *Changing Your Diet: Choosing Nutrient-rich Foods - familydoctor.org.* Familydoctor.org. https://familydoctor.org/changing-your-diet-choosing-nutrient-rich-foods/

Flottum, K. (2015, January 29). *Beekeeping 101: Supplies, Plans and How To.* Popular Mechanics. https://www.popularmechanics.com/home/lawn-garden/how-to/g56/diy-backyard-beekeeping-47031701/

Great Benefits of Homesteading. (2014, January 21). The Elliott Homestead. https://theelliotthomestead.com/2014/01/great-benefits-of-homesteading/

Harvard Health Publishing. (2019, February 6). *The best foods for vitamins and minerals - Harvard Health.* Harvard Health. https://www.health.harvard.edu/staying-healthy/the-best-foods-for-vitamins-and-minerals

History.com Editors. (2018, August 21). *Homestead Act.* HISTORY. https://www.history.com/topics/american-civil-war/homestead-act

Home Wind Power: Yes, in My Backyard! | MOTHER EARTH NEWS. (2014). Mother Earth News.

https://www.motherearthnews.com/renewable-energy/wind-power/home-wind-power-zm0z13amzrob

Homestead exemption. (2021, February 2). Wikipedia. https://en.wikipedia.org/wiki/Homestead_exemption

Homestead Exemption Rules and Regulations. (n.d.). **Www.dor.ms.gov**. https://www.dor.ms.gov/Pages/Homestead-Rules.aspx

Homestead Goats - What You Need to Know to Get Started. (2016, December 9). Common Sense Home. https://commonsensehome.com/homestead-goats/

Housing Your Chickens: All You Need to Know to Do It Properly. (2018, December 20). MorningChores. https://morningchores.com/chicken-housing/

How Does Solar Power Work | Solar Power Experts. (n.d.). Infinite Energy. https://www.infiniteenergy.com.au/about-solar-power/how-solar-power-works/

How Does Solar Work? (n.d.). Energy.gov. https://www.energy.gov/eere/solar/how-does-solar-work

How to Build a Raised Bed CHEAP and EASY, Backyard Gardening. (n.d.). **Www.youtube.com**. https://www.youtube.com/watch?app=desktop&v=MBIYebUgVVI

How to Install Outdoor Electric Wiring. (n.d.). WikiHow. https://www.wikihow.com/Install-Outdoor-Electric-Wiring

How to Make Soap at Home (Even if You Failed Chemistry). (2020, August 12). Food52. https://food52.com/blog/12919-how-to-make-soap-at-home-even-if-you-failed-chemistry

How to Sell Backyard Chicken Eggs. (2017, May 8). The Happy Chicken Coop. https://www.thehappychickencoop.com/how-to-sell-backyard-chicken-eggs/

How to Sell Meat Legally as Part of Your Homestead Business. (n.d.). Www.youtube.com. https://www.youtube.com/watch?app=desktop&v=Ix O9GweZDEM

How to Sell Your Honey and Beeswax Harvest. (2019, August 11). MorningChores. https://morningchores.com/how-to-sell-honey-and-beeswax/

How to Stay Grounded and Centered in Life: 6 Techniques. (2020, June 6). Put the Kettle On. https://putthekettleon.ca/how-to-stay-grounded-and-centered-in-life/

How to stretch a fence. (n.d.). **Www.youtube.com**. https://www.youtube.com/watch?app=desktop&v=tk SPejY7g-U

Hydroponics at Home. (n.d.). **Www.youtube.com**. https://www.youtube.com/watch?app=desktop&v=1o ETmA6AJQk

Jan 30, F. | H. 3040 | U., & Print, 2020 |. (2020, January 30). *Canning Foods at Home*. Home & Garden Information Center | Clemson University, South

Carolina. https://hgic.clemson.edu/factsheet/canning-foods-at-home/

Krista, A. (2020, August 15). *Dehydrating Foods for Storage: An Essential Homesteading Skill*. Goose Creek Homestead. https://goosecreekhomestead.com/dehydrating-foods-for-storage/

Leigh. (n.d.). *Mindset: Key To Successful Homesteading?* 5 Acres and a Dream. https://www.5acresandadream.com/2011/01/mindset-key-to-successful-homesteading.html

Link, R. (2017). *The 14 Healthiest Vegetables on Earth*. Healthline. https://www.healthline.com/nutrition/14-healthiest-vegetables-on-earth

Lovely Greens. (2013, September 20). Lovely Greens. https://lovelygreens.com/natural-soapmaking-for-beginners/

Makena, W. (n.d.). *How to succeed in the dried fruits business*. The Standard. https://www.standardmedia.co.ke/hustle/article/2001324409/how-to-succeed-in-the-dried-fruits-business

Making Soil Blocks. (n.d.). Www.youtube.com. https://www.youtube.com/watch?app=desktop&v=xLbAkqau_MI

McCoy, D. (2019, November 25). *10 Essential Crops for a Self Sufficient Garden*. The Rustic Elk. https://www.therusticelk.com/self-sufficient-garden/

Mubitana, S. (2017, December 8). *How to Start a Dried Fruits Business*. Smatfin. https://smatfin.com/how-to-start-a-dried-fruits-business/

North, D. (2016, May 30). *What is Aquaponics and How Does it Work?* The Permaculture Research Institute. https://www.permaculturenews.org/2016/05/30/what-is-aquaponics-and-how-does-it-work/

Reynolds, M. (n.d.). *Build a Backyard Bee House*. DIY. https://www.diynetwork.com/how-to/outdoors/gardening/build-a-backyard-bee-house

seamsterFollow. (n.d.). *Build a Simple Shed: a Complete Guide*. Instructables. Retrieved https://www.instructables.com/Build-a-simple-shed-a-complete-guide/

Self-watering SIP Sub-irrigated Raised Bed Construction (How to Build). (2015, April 29). Www.youtube.com. https://www.youtube.com/watch?app=desktop&v=Lp9Jdyno9hI

Setting a fence post. (n.d.). Www.youtube.com. https://www.youtube.com/watch?app=desktop&v=9D2H_xq78Mw

Smoking Meat 101 - [Complete Guide] Smoking & Types of Smokers. (2018, March 7). Smoking Meat Geeks | #MeatGeeks. https://smokingmeatgeeks.com/smoking-meat-basics/

Superstore, R. (n.d.). *Re-roof your shed roof: A DIY Guide*. Roofing Superstore Help & Advice. https://www.roofingsuperstore.co.uk/help-and-advice/product-guides/pitched-roofing/reroof-your-shed-roof/

Tamara, N. (n.d.). *50 Essential Crops to Grow in Your Survival Garden*. Https://Crisisequipped.com/. https://crisisequipped.com/crops-to-grow-in-your-survival-garden/

The Easiest Way To Make Any Homemade Fruit Jam (feat. Krewella). (n.d.). Www.youtube.com. https://www.youtube.com/watch?app=desktop&v=KUGjgUA-BWU

Top 10 Homestead Crops. (2020, December 4). Mary's Heirloom Seeds. https://www.marysheirloomseeds.com/blogs/news/top-10-homestead-crops

verticalroots. (2020, March 3). *What is hydroponic farming? Why use hydroponics?* Vertical Roots. https://www.verticalroots.com/the-what-and-why-of-hydroponic-farming/

Vivian, J. (n.d.). *The Secrets of Low-Tech Plumbing*. Mother Earth News. https://www.motherearthnews.com/homesteading-and-livestock/low-tech-plumbing-zmaz95jjztak

We've Broken Down the Science of Composting for You. (n.d.). Better Homes & Gardens. https://www.bhg.com/gardening/yard/compost/how-to-compost/

What is Aquaponics. (2019). The Aquaponic Source. https://www.theaquaponicsource.com/what-is-aquaponics/

Why You Should Have Goats on Your Homestead. (n.d.). Oak Hill Homestead. https://www.oakhillhomestead.com/2014/03/why-you-should-have-goats-on-your.html

Winger, J. (2015, January 2). *7 Reasons to Start Homesteading Today*. The Prairie Homestead. https://www.theprairiehomestead.com/2015/01/start-homesteading-today.html

Market Gardening

Step-By-Step Guide to Start Your Own Small Scale Organic Farm in as Little as 30 Days With the Most Up-To-Date Information

Small Footprint Press

Introduction

"Growing Your Own Food is Like Printing Your Own Money"

-Ron Finley

For many, buying a little house on wide stretches of land is a dream. People want to escape the non-stop hustle of city living and the exhausting days of working just for a paycheck. They want something more fulfilling to put their time, effort, and money into. There are many reasons why you may want to start your own farm and just as many reasons why you haven't yet. Maybe you do not have the money or the land. Maybe you have attempted to start small and saw nothing flourish from your efforts, and this keeps you from trying again.

You might be here because you are passionate about growing your own foods and creating a self-sustainable life. Perhaps you want to finally break free of the nine to five or 60 hour or more workweeks for a job that leaves you stressed and often depressed. Maybe the idea of having your own farm, whether to grow enough to feed your family or sell to generate an income, has been dancing around in your head for a while. With this in mind, you'll probably want to know how to take this thought and turn it into a reality, and a successful one at that.

If you don't know what you are getting into, it is easy to fail at starting your own farm. Some of you may have experienced this failure already with unsuccessful growing seasons. However, you can have the motivation, determination, and passion to try again and learn from your mistakes. You will just need to know the proper steps to take.

Farming is not for everyone. If you are looking for a quick way to earn a few extra bucks, this book may not be for you. If you just want tips to cut corners for fast, overnight results, you will not learn any of that on these pages. However, those who are willing to take action, put in the required effort, and make a commitment to continuously learn and grow as a farmer will find value in this book. This book was designed for people like you, with passion, drive, and a willingness to learn.

Small Footprint Press was created out of the same passion and drive that you have. We are a company dedicated to helping others learn how to live off their land by taking care of mother earth and its inhabitants. We are a team of enthusiastic professionals who have poured out time and effort into studying and reaching out to experts on sustainable living, prepping, living off-grid to create guides for individuals who are inspired to change their lifestyles. In addition, we have a love for all things outdoors, especially when it comes to building a better earth. It is from our passion that we feel compelled to share these amazing messages and information with others.

In the past year, we have been formulating books on the information we have collected from experts and our own research, on how to achieve a sustainable lifestyle that can allow any individual and their environment to thrive. Watching people in this world provide for themselves and their loved ones fills us with excitement. Seeing them accomplish their goals and living their purpose by creating their own farming business is what inspires us to get out of bed and help others to do the same. This is why we have carefully crafted this book, to help more people see the potential of their land and learn how to successfully care for it, so it may continue to give back for years.

The information in this book will provide you with a better insight into how to turn your small farm into a reliable source of income. Whether it is an acre, ten acres, or more, you will learn how you can grow and profit from what you have. There is so much more to operating a farm than just the crops and harvest. There are legal issues you can run into if you do not know what your small farming business needs. You will learn what insurance, permits, and other documents are necessary to run your farm legally. You will also have to learn about the marketing aspect of things and how you can better transform your passion into a business.

This book is not filled with information to read and forget. Instead, you will learn effective action plans that you can implement immediately. These plans are flexible and will provide you the structure, knowledge, and systems to grow a successful business. The sooner you get started, the sooner you will benefit, so let's start now. It is time to take the first step towards that dream of farm living you have always had.

Chapter 1:
Establishing Roots

Learning as much as you can from the beginning will put you in a position to make better, well-educated decisions on the operations of your farm. Effectively working on your farm will be lucrative, but it's easy to lose sight of important matters. So have patience and give yourself some credit as you embark on this journey. You will not become a master of every skill you need all at once. And at times no matter how much you plan and prepare, some things will not work out perfectly the first time.

Rule Number One

Starting any business is a risk. While some businesses have lower risks, they can all lead to stress and financial strain. One of the things that you'll want to avoid is getting yourself in debt with no clear expectation of when you will make your initial investment back and start generating a profit. Deciding to start your own farm is highly rewarding, but without the right plan, it can cause you to lose a significant amount of money.

Avoiding Debt

The startup cost for a new farmer will vary depending on what you already have to work with. If you already have the land, your cost of starting a farm can fall around

$40,000, but most of these costs are essential investments that will make it possible for you to create a profit sooner, such as purchasing the right equipment. There are plenty of options for financing your small-scale farm, but even with funding, you need to spend wisely.

Spending sensibly requires you to make a budget and a plan. With these two components, you will make financial choices that get your agricultural business going without sinking into debt. For many beginners, this will mean having a great deal of patience. You will have to weigh the pros and cons of the many options you'll have at the beginning. You have to carefully consider the choices that will benefit you temporarily and those that will help you expand and reach your long-term goals sooner.

You may have to settle with used or borrowed equipment, ask family or friends for help, and research on how to do a lot of things yourself to save on money. This will keep you in safe financial standing. You never want to start spending money on things you can hold off on until you have enough capital to cover your overhead. Unfortunately, this may mean owning your own farm might have to be put on hold until you come up with your own savings to get started. This is a much better option. While you are saving, you can do the research and learn in the meantime, so that when you have the funds, you'll have a plan already in mind.

Incurring debt may be inevitable, and we will discuss funding options in greater detail in the next chapter. There are some ways to avoid getting stuck with a substantial amount of debt before you begin looking at your investment options. First, understand what types of debt you may encounter. These include:

- Secured

- Unsecured

- Fixed interest rates

- Variable interest rates

- Fixed payment term

- Variable payment term

- Deductible loans

- Non-deductible loans

Each of these has its own pros and cons. Choosing the right fit for your business will require a thorough evaluation of the direction you want your farm to go. Of course, being profitable is the main goal, but how you get there will influence the type of debt you might consider. A few things to avoid when it comes to choosing the right funding include:

- High-interest rates

- High late fees or penalties

- Obtaining a debt for things that will not increase your value or for things that have a short lifespan

- Relying too much on secured debt

- Unverified lending sources

- Obtaining debt that requires a monthly payment that is more than 36 percent of your gross monthly income

Don't Learn The Hard Way.

It is okay to fail in some things. You will learn through the process. Amazingly, those in the agriculture industry like small farmers experience a much lower failure rate than those starting a business in the restaurant or other industries. This may or may not happen to you, but there are ways to make your chances better, by avoiding mistakes that have led others to fail. The following are things to be aware of as you begin and avoid as you continue to embark on this journey.

- Remember, your farm is your business. A mistake many beginners make is allowing the ideal of a farming lifestyle to impair their business sense. While the idea of growing your own food and maybe even raising some animals may look picturesque, this is not how you approach starting a successful business. As a business person, you need to carefully consider your market, profit margins, and products. You don't want to just grow some plants. You'll want to grow crops that you can sell, and this means you know what people want to buy that you can supply them. When you decide to start a farm, you will need to be clear as to whether you will be treating it like a business or a hobby.

- Easy and cheap will not build a sustainable business. As a beginner, it will be tempting to choose crops that are quick and easy to harvest and then turn around and sell these for a very low profit to compete against bigger chains. You may find a little bit of success with this approach, but most will waste a lot of time and energy only to achieve minimal success if any.

- Choose the right market. This connects to the first two points. You are operating a business, and to be successful, you will need to market to the right customer. You will need to see those who will be willing to spend on your produce and who will not just be looking for the lowest price. You do not want to compete with the local chain stores to sell your produce. It won't be possible for a small-scale farmer to capitalize on the same strategies as these chains. Instead, you will need to select profitable crops that are in demand and customers are willing to buy.

- Gain at least a basic understanding of your day-to-day accounting. If you have the means to hire an account, even better, but if it is only possible to handle the bigger financial obligation like taxes, then you will need to handle the accounting on your own. As a new business, it is vital to have a budget and know where your money is coming from and going towards. Do not get into the habit of buying your supplies without tracking what you are spending. By the end of the month, you will often have to sort out how bills and necessities will be paid the following month while still having to pay things off from the current month. You will have to understand what your cost of business is to understand what profits are possible.

- Have cash reserves. Farming is just like any other business, and you will be bound to encounter issues that will hit you hard financially. If you do not have a little cushion to get you through these hard hits, you will be completely out.

- Do not try to do everything. Have a clear vision of what you want for your farm and resist the urge to constantly have more, offer more, and undoubtedly will cost more. You will have to maintain a focus on what will turn the greatest profits, not what looks appealing, or you do not have any real interest in profiting.

- Do not try to mimic other successful farms unless you have a clear understanding of what makes them successful. Every farmer will have their own systems, marketing plan, and ways of doing business that have led them to success. Trying to copy what another farm is doing because they have had success does not mean you will have success. Most often, this will run right into failure. This does not mean you can not look to other well-established farmers for guidance or inspiration, but if you are trying to obtain the success of a farmer that produces grapes and apples while you are growing spinach and radish, you will not get the same results. If you want to implement what another farm is doing, first understand what it takes to implement that system. You might not be at the size or have the means to pursue that option yet.

Know Your Market

How long should you wait until you begin marketing your future farm? You should not wait at all. If you are serious about establishing a successful business, you will need to start marketing that business before you even have the crops growing in the fields.

Marketing is grossly neglected by many farmers who are just starting out, and this is often the main reason their business grows only minimally, if at all. This is also the one aspect of business that intimidates entrepreneurs in many industries. If marketing makes you cringe, it is understandable. Many people have the wrong impression of what marketing is and should entail. Marketing your farm and products is not just about selling, which is where most entrepreneurs go wrong with their marketing approach. They try to push their products on people until they buy, and this is ineffective.

Marketing should be about sharing. Knowing what to share requires an understanding of your target market, but more importantly, it requires you to know why this is important to you. You do not need to have your farm yet. You do not need to be harvesting or packaging or anywhere near ready to start selling items. What you need is, to be honest and open about why you are starting a farm, what you want to gain, how you want to provide for your community and for your family. Sharing these personal reasons will attract the right people to your business. One important thing to do is to create a personality or branding that people can emotionally connect to. This should be done so that your customers won't see you only like a hungry salesman who only cares about making money, but as a human being that they can relate to, will want to listen to, and will want to support.

Market Now, Not Later

Starting to share your story now creates interest and excitement about your future farm. You share with a few family and friends, start a social media page and share your journey with new followers, and before long, you'll have hundreds and maybe even thousands of people invested in your business. Although this can be a scary thought, these people will be following your journey as you make progress. They will feel like they are right there with you.

If you start marketing right away, you will begin to build strong relationships, and this creates loyal customers. Being transparent about your process will allow people to trust what you eventually end up providing. Sharing, instead of selling, allows people to follow along with you and learn more about who you are as a person, why this is important to you, and will allow them to start realizing that this is important to them too. For example, sharing that you are passionate about growing organic items because you want to eliminate potential chemicals you may be feeding to your family when you purchase store-bought, big chain produce will get followers rethinking what they feed to their families. Talking about how your small farm will have a positive impact on the environment will get people thinking about supporting local farmers more.

There are many topics you can cover and share that can resonate with your followers. Getting a headstart on this before you even have products to sell will ensure that you attract more than enough people who will then be just as passionate about seeing you succeed as you are. You can gain a great deal of support when you begin marketing by sharing first, instead of waiting to market just to sell. People are going to buy from what or who they know. By sharing your values or backstory, you can become someone they know personally and you can get a bump to the top of their buy-from list.

Social media has made it easier than ever to begin sharing now and gain attention. There are many ways you can approach social media marketing with your small farm. Each social media platform, like YouTube, Facebook, Instagram, and Twitter, have their own set of pros and cons. Each tends to cater to a specific demographic of users, and certain content, such as videos, images, or written text. Thus, each platform will perform differently. Obviously, YouTube is meant for video creators, while Facebook is ideal for those who can combine different types of content into one post.

You should start your plan on creating your social media accounts for your farming business now. You can begin with just one or two platforms to share regularly. You will also want to set up an email list and website and create a way to capture contact info for visitors. This will feel like a lot in the beginning as it can quickly become overwhelming, especially when you start adding all the daily tasks of preparing the land. But this is a vital component for your success. Creating a marketing or social media schedule will help you organize what you need to do daily and will allow you allocate a set time for getting these marketing responsibilities done.

Know Your Land

This topic will be more thoroughly discussed in Chapter 5, but it is something many farmers feel the need to have in order first. To have a successful small farming business, you will need to have reliable land to grow on. Your land is a crucial component. You will need to know how much you have to work with. If you need to buy land, you will have to know where to find it and how much it will cost.

Additionally, you will want to know what crops will grow best, where, and when. You will want to consider how to create a profit from year-round crops. Then, there are rotating crops, soil, fertilizing, and so much more. Before you begin to take all of these things into consideration, you will need to know your market first. Solving all of the resource issues before you know who is going to buy from you will save you a lot of wasted effort and time.

Setting Realistic Goals

You cannot leave things up to chance when starting your business, and what many beginners tend to do is not treat their farming endeavor as a business. If you want to generate a profit from your farm, then you will need to treat it as a business. Setting goals is a must, but simply creating a plan is still less than half of the process. Although anyone can set a goal, very few accomplish it. This is because the initial excitement they have when they start and first set their big or small goals diminishes as they start putting in the work to accomplish them. They let temptation and distraction pull them in different directions, and after a few weeks or months, their goals are long forgotten. You cannot rely on excitement alone when it comes to success. You need to have a deep internal factor that motivates you and pushes you to do the things you need to do even when you do not feel like doing them. This is what will set you apart from the hundreds of other farmers starting out.

Align Goals With Your Passion

Passion is what will keep you motivated through the ups and downs of this adventure. Without passion, you will have no purpose. Without purpose, you will let any little thing keep you from completing the priority task that will get your farm and business running. If farming is not something you are truly invested in, without profit expectation, this might not be the right course for you. You will need to be passionate about growing your own foods, taking care of the land, and seeing your efforts in a bigger scheme, such as providing food to those living in your community. You will need this passion to drive you through long, physically demanding days. This passion will get you through unexpected setbacks, like when mother nature rolls in and wipes out half your crops. Finally, you will need this passion to keep you aligned with what is most important to you instead of finding quick fixes and temporary wins.

There are many reasons why you think farming is the right path for you. However, some of the most common reasons people start their own small farming business are:

- Love for the land and farming.

- Increasing knowledge about organic foods.

- Growing your own foods for self-sufficient and sustainable living.

- Providing job opportunities or educating others.

Your reason will have a direct impact on how you set and achieve your business goals. Your "why" will be a determining factor for the processes you use on your farm and will influence daily and future operations. Before you start planning on how to layout your crops or where to sell and before you make any investment, ask yourself why it is important to have your own farm. Then ask yourself honestly if this is going to be a good enough reason to push you to put in the effort. Many people start off with the greatest intentions, but once they start putting in the work, they realize that this is not the best fit for them. Be clear about why you want to get started; think about the impact this will have on your life both now and in the future. If the desire to create change and start your own farm consistently outweighs the fears and reluctance, then this might be worth you pursuing.

If you are uncertain, then get some real-life experience working on a farm if you do not have some already. Once you know what you are getting yourself into, you will find it easier to make certain choices.

Set Reasonable Goals

After you have established your "why," you need to start thinking about how you can get there. SMART goals will keep you motivated, focused, and successful. Everyone sets yearly goals and then quickly stashes them away and forgets about them. Operating a business requires you to keep your goals in focus. You should set yearly, monthly, weekly, and even daily goals. Accomplishing your daily goals will enable you to achieve your weekly goals, and conquering your weekly goals makes your monthly goals achievable. It is always important to keep your purpose in mind as you are setting your goals, both big and small. Having the end goals in mind, you will begin to create a list of goals you need to achieve to get there. For each goal you set, you will want them to meet each of the following criteria.

- Specific: Your goal must establish who is involved, what you want to accomplish, what you need to do to accomplish, and why accomplishing this is important.

- Measurable: A measurable goal gives you something to track. If you have nothing to track, you have nothing to show your progress.

- Achievable: Goals need to be realistic, within your budget, and something you are willing and able to put in the effort to achieve.

- Relevant: Goals need to relate to your purpose. There needs to be a reason for why this goal is important to achieve so that it moves you toward your desired end results. This factor is important because many people make the mistake of setting certain goals because they think they have to. Everyone else is doing it, so you must do it too. This can result in a lot of wasted time trying to achieve something that has no positive impact on what you are actually trying to gain; they just serve as a distraction.

- Timely: You will need to set a deadline to achieve your goals. Open-ended goals are often not achieved or procrastinated on. When you have a deadline, you will ensure that you are doing the things that need to be done in that timeframe.

When you have gone through all of the above, you should be left with clear and concise goals that tell you exactly what you want to achieve, how you are going to achieve them, and when it will be done. From these goals, you can create a plan that consists of small steps or milestones to accomplish daily, weekly, and monthly, so that you can make sure that all your goals will be met.

Before you start taking action on these, you will need to prioritize them. Carefully review your goals and identify the ones that have the biggest influence on your long-term goals. Also, keep in mind that you should be working on the goals that are most important to you and your well-being.

After you have prioritized your goals, you need to start taking action. This is where many begin to fail. After you have gone through the effort and daunting task of creating the goals, which may have taken more effort than you thought, you now need to put them into motion. Start with one of your top three goals. Break it down into daily manageable steps. Pick one thing you can begin doing today to help you accomplish it. Each day, choose one thing to accomplish. Once you get into the habit of making it a non-negotiable to get that one thing done, begin to choose two things, then three. As you begin to take action, remember: it is important to track your progress. Be sure to keep a record of what you are doing each day. At the end of each week, review your progress. Identify what is working for you, what you need to work on more, or what needs to be done differently. And then, with that knowledge, create a plan for the next week on how you can implement the necessary changes.

Taking this approach to your goals may seem slow. However, each task you complete will add up to your major personal or professional accomplishments. Keep in mind also that the small, consistent steps you take to start your farming business or create change will compound. Just as you cannot force a seed to grow into a fruit-bearing tree overnight, you cannot expect your goals to produce results overnight. However, if you consistently nourish that seed, provide it with water, sunlight, and the proper growing environment, eventually it will begin to grow. And from there, you will have a healthy tree-bearing fruit for weeks. Treat your goals as the seed that will flourish into the life you dream of, but they will only do so when you commit to taking care of the steps and tasks that need to be done.

Chapter 2:
Understand the Risk
vs. Reward

This chapter is dedicated to helping you gain clarity over what you are getting into when you start a new business. After this chapter, we'll dive into all the ins and outs of what you need to get started, followed by the legal concerns and lending options which can be overwhelming. By first recognizing the pros and cons, you will find that all the other aspects are just part of the business. You do not want to jump into this adventure without properly assessing whether this is the best fit for you. There will be ups and downs, hard choices to make, and you may feel disappointed that your progress is not moving as quickly as you like. However, if this is something you are passionate about pursuing, these will just be hiccups in your journey.

Honestly assess what you care about getting into. You will want to ensure that a small-scale farm is something you want and will enjoy doing. You do not want to start this type of project without understanding the full commitment that needs to be made. Otherwise, you will waste time and realize too late that this is not the right adventure for you. Carefully review the information in this chapter before moving forward.

The Pros

Farming may be in your blood, and that will make it easier to see the benefits of pursuing a farming business. If it is not, you find many aspects of owning a farm appealing. Farming is highly rewarding to those who seek a different way of living, one that allows them to set their own rules and live more independently. There are plenty of other beneficial reasons for starting your own farm as well.

Welcome to Entrepreneurship

When you start and operate your own farm, you are officially a business owner. You become your own boss. As your own boss, you get to organize and establish the rules. All the control and executive decisions are made by you. Being your own boss gives you more opportunities to advance your skills, gain more experiences, and grow professionally and personally.

The work you do will be all the more satisfying despite still being hard. There is also no limitation on how much you can earn. While there is no guarantee that you will turn profits every quarter, there is also nothing standing in your way of exceeding your expected earnings. At any time, depending on the success of your farm, you can decide to give yourself a raise or a nice paid week vacation!

Maintain a Healthier Lifestyle

You know that fueling your body with nourishing whole foods is beneficial to your physical and mental health. Many people get into farming because they want to ensure that the foods they eat and feed their families are free of chemicals. Farming provides them the assurance that what they are putting into their body is of the best quality. This desire can expand to wanting to make quality fresh foods more easily available to others.

Having your own farms ensures that you always have a supply of healthy food for you and your family free of charge. Whatever you grow, you can use it for meals in your own home. There will usually never seem to be a shortage of fresh fruits or vegetables. Growing a surplus of these items lets you stay aligned with a healthy lifestyle while also making it a possibility for others too.

Predictable Demand

There will always be a need for farmers and crops, and this demand is continuously growing. There are 7.5 billion people living around the world, and the global population is expected to reach 9.7 billion by 2050 (Elferink and Schierhorn, 2016). There are more people than there are farms growing food to meet the demand and need for produce. Even if you live in a small populated area, the people there are still in need of fresh produce, and you can be their supply chain. If you also take into consideration that the restaurants in your area also need fresh food supplies, rest assured that there will always be a demand for produce that your farm can definitely meet. This can take out the risk and uncertainty of whether your business will be a success. Unlike many other businesses who need to cater to a niched-down target audience and are also in competition with the next best thing, you do not have to worry about your business being taken out because of any fancy upgrades being developed. Your crops will stay as a necessity of life, and there will not be many ways you can modify or improve what you grow aside from the other items you may create with your crops like sauces or jams.

Easy Diversification

When you own land, there are many options for generating an income. Growing crops and selling what you harvest is the most obvious and best-starting place. However, once you have gained the experience from a few growing seasons, you might be thinking about other ways you can expand your small farm business to create more income streams. This can be adding livestock to your farm, providing tours, allowing people to pick their own fruits and vegetables for a fee, writing cookbooks using only the crop you grow, providing an online educational resource in the form of books or a blog, selling sauces, fresh baked goods, spices, seasonings, dressing, and other homemade packaged foods. The possibilities are endless! Don't be afraid to think outside the box when looking for ways to diversify your farm, but do keep your excitement under control. You do not want to add more than you can handle or will be profitable.

Gratitude and Life Satisfaction

Operating your own farm will keep you in the heart of nature. You will witness life cycles and gain a greater appreciation for all that surrounds you. Once you have gotten through the first year and most of the fear and risk has subsided, you will reach a flow in your farming business. You'll appreciate the hard work and understand that this diligence does not just benefit you, it benefits your direct environment and community. Would you rather be sitting in morning rush hours listening to the insidious sounds of beeping horns and screeching tires, or would you rather have a fresh cup of coffee out in the field listening to the calming early sounds of nature? The work environment, co-workers, and job expectations of working on a farm are vastly different from those of a typical nine to five office job.

Every day on the job is different. While some tasks may grow mundane, you will find that you have something new to do every day. These may be new challenges to overcome or problems to solve, but no two days will be the same, and you will never get bored. Instead, you always feel like you have been productive and that what you are putting your time and energy into is serving a bigger purpose.

There is also the simple fact that most people find more satisfaction growing their own foods. You nurture your seeds from the very beginning, and in the end, you get to enjoy the product of your hard work. When you harvest your first crop and bring in a basket of fresh vegetables or fruits to create a meal, you have a greater sense of pride in your accomplishments.

Create Better Habits

Those who are self-employed quickly learn that to reach their goals working for themselves, they need to have the right habits. You will quickly learn how to adopt better habits that will increase your productivity and motivation. For example, being your own boss will push you to become more disciplined and diligent because if you aren't, your business will fall. While this can be a scary thought, many farmers use this as motivation. In return, they get to enjoy a life with more flexibility and independence.

The Cons

Though there is a lot to be gained from starting your own farm, there will be challenges. Knowing that you are going to have obstacles to overcome and being honest about your ability to stick it out and overcome them is a crucial determining factor to consider. There are many things that will be out of your control as you begin farming, and many of these things cause farmers to turn around and head back to their safer way of living. However, if you can embrace the challenges, work through them, and not let them deter you from your grand vision in life, farming may be the right business adventure to start. But, first, it is important to know what these challenges will be.

Mother Nature

Mother nature is not always going to work with you, but you still need to work. Some days are going to be freezing, pouring down rain, or extremely hot. Despite what the weather is looking like that day, you will still need to get up and head to the fields. On days where the weather keeps you indoors, you will need to accept that the next day of work is going to be four times as hard and at least twice as long. You will need to be ready for disappointment when there are long days without rain or a sudden late-season frost.

You can be more adaptable to weather when you stay aware of the weather forecast. Making it a habit to check the forecast daily and prepare your farm for certain weather predictions will minimize the damage caused.

Additionally, educating yourself about the season and climate changes is essential. Having a clear understanding of when you can expect lots of rain or lack of it will allow you to begin to manage these issues well before they happen.

The Workday Feels Like It Never Ends

There will be a lot of hard labour to do, especially at the beginning. Even when you are not tending to your crops, there will always be equipment needing repaired, marketing done, people to call back, and the list can feel never-ending. You might even find yourself going to bed and suddenly realizing that you've forgotten five other things. So then you'll have to get out of bed and get things done, despite being exhausted already. Starting any type of business will be demanding, but a farm is more physically and mentally draining day in and day out. Until you have established yourself and harvested your first successful crop, you will feel as if you're working 24 hours a day. However, once that crop is harvested and you see the return on your efforts, everything will be well worth it.

Everything Is Your Responsibility

You are the boss. This means you will need to be aware and on top of everything before it goes wrong or gets worse. You will need to be focused and pay attention to what is going on around you. You will have to motivate yourself to work when you do not feel like it, wake up early, and work late even if you'd rather be relaxing on the couch. Farming also requires investing the time to educate yourself. Learning all the legalities and food standards is not going to be a particularly fun aspect of farming, but if you want to be successful, you will seek out opportunities to learn more about the industry. There is a lot that can go wrong, and these things can be costly. Pests can overtake your crops in a day, leaving you with nothing to harvest. Flooding can destroy your soil, so you have nothing to plant in. There are things that are going to be out of your control, but with the right planning and determination, you will remain in control of the things you can control. This will lead you to become highly successful.

Financial Concerns

As you get started growing, there will be more expenses than profits. Many people who are just getting started on their farming business find themselves needing to keep their reliable day job or have to pick up a second job to pay the bills. It can be a struggle in the first one or two years to make time to complete all the farm chores. Expect a lot of late nights and early mornings. Despite the financial stress in the beginning, those who power through the first year or two agree that the struggles of the first few years were well worth it.

Weighing Your Options

Now that you have a better idea of the pros and cons, ask yourself if this is the right fit for you. When you weigh the pros and cons against each other, the pros should significantly outweigh the cons. If you are still uncertain, you might want to try a much smaller endeavor. Having your own farm is highly rewarding and can be a profitable option to pursue, but you will need to understand that the excitement you might be feeling in the beginning will wear off once you start getting to work. Ask yourself and answer the following questions honestly before you move forward.

- Do you picture yourself maintaining your farm one year from now? Five years from now? Are you still waking up and heading to the fields every day?

- Do you have the resources to start your farm? If not, how will you find the resources? Also, be honest about how motivated you are to seek out the right resources to guarantee your farm's success.

- Are you willing to learn what is necessary for growing a successful business and farm?

- How much time are you willing to dedicate to caring for your farm?

- How long have you been waiting to start your own farming business? Is this a new interest or a passion you have been putting off for years?

- Have you ever volunteered on a farm? If not, it's a good idea to do so to get hands-on experience for what to expect.

- How much do financial gains influence your decision to start a farm? If this is the main reason, this is not going to be the right business for you.

If you still feel hesitation, it might be better to wait. Maybe you are really passionate about sustainable living and organic farming, but the amount of work it will take is not something you are willing to commit to for the long term.

Maybe you have reservations about the upfront cost of starting a farm and need more time to evaluate your goals. It is understandable why you may still be uncertain about starting your own farming business, and this might come down to the fact that you do not see yourself as a business owner. Growing your own crops and making a profit does require you to shift your mindset to one that is optimistic and empowering. If you had attempted to start a crop before and did not see success, you might have adopted the mindset that you have already failed once, and you don't want to fail again. It is important that through this whole journey, you check in with yourself regularly. Be sure that your passion is still pushing you and that mistakes or unsuccessful attempts are not defining you.

Keep yourself grounded as well. Another mistake you can make when you have the idea to start your own farm is focusing too much on the big picture. It can be easy to let excitement convince you that you can take on much more than you have planned out for the beginning. You want to go big or go home right from the start. While having big goals and dreams is not discouraged, you also need to remain grounded. Wanting to jump right into having a large farm with various crops, you are going to burn out quickly and give up. Instead, start small, learn from the process, discover what works and does not work for you, and then go bigger. If you have never farmed before, there will be a lot of lessons to learn during the first few years, and you will continue learning as you continue growing. If you are willing to keep learning and growing, then a small-scale farm might be the right fit for you.

Chapter 3:
Gathering the Essentials

After deciding you want to move forward with your farming business, you will have to know what you need and begin to gather the tools, equipment, and other essentials necessary for operating your farm. You won't need to go out and purchase brand-new items. Starting out, you can save some of your time and money by researching on your own and buying or borrow used tools. Getting experience using certain types of equipment will help you decide what to invest in for future growth. In this chapter, there will be a wide selection of gear to acquire to get you started, but this is not an exhaustive list. You may find that as you begin, you will need other tools or equipment to make the process better suit you and your needs. The items mentioned here are suggestions, and you will have to choose whether to invest or not. But you should know what you will be investing in if you decide to do so. You need to create a budget for these items, and these items will often need some funding to help you get started.

Land

If you do not already have much land to farm on, this is going to be the biggest part of your investment. If you are looking for land that will also serve as your residence, then it can be easier to find suitable acreage to get started, but you will have to take into account that this can result in a sizable mortgage.

If you do not have land, there are plenty of ways for you to obtain farmland. Some places to begin your search include:

- The Land Connection
- LoopNet
- Shared Earth
- Farm Lease Pro
- LandandFarm
- AgriSeek

You can also find information about land for sale or lease in your area or state by visiting the International Farm Transition Network website or FindAFarmer website. The price you pay for land will vary by location. On average, you can anticipate paying around 3,000 dollars per acre.

Seeds

Knowing when and where to buy seeds will save you money and ensure you will have enough to get your crops started. In addition, it is important to keep in mind what season you will be growing in. Your farm will be more successful if you have a mix of cold and warm weather crops.

You need to find reputable and trustworthy seed suppliers. You can often find a local business to purchase your seeds from, but you might find more varieties by going with an online supplier. It is important to do your research on the seller to ensure that you will get quality seeds and that they are what they are supposed to be, especially for organic seeds. Some online businesses to consider:

- American Meadows- Great selection of wildflower seeds

- Clear Creek Seed- Best for heirloom seeds, but also have vegetable, herb, and flower seeds.

- Fedco Seeds- Plenty of organic seeds options, but also has a variety of trees, vegetables, and exotic seeds.

- Pinetree Garden Seed (superseeds.com)- Offers easy-to-grow seeds, organic, heirloom, and flower seeds

- Nourse Farms- High-quality strawberry, raspberry, blackberry, and blueberry plants

- Seed Savers Exchange- Offers endangered variety seeds and rare heirloom seeds

- Seeds of Change- Nice selection of organic seeds

- High Mowing Organic Seeds- Best for certified organic seeds

- Sow True Seed- Has over 500 organic and heirloom seeds to choose from

- Renee's Garden- Best for international hybrids and exotic seeds

- Baker Creek Heirloom Seeds- Best for rare seeds

- Botanical Interests- Nice selection of all types of seeds such as heirloom, organic, and non-GMO

- Southern Exposure Seed Exchange- Best for a wide selection of tomatoes, but also has a nice selection of other vegetable seeds

- Johnny's Selected Seeds- Nice selection of high-quality vegetable and flower seeds

- Territorial Seed Company- Offers over 48 varieties of lettuce seeds and also has other vegetables, herb, and flower seeds

- Sustainable Seed Company- Great selection of vegetable, heirloom, and organic certified seeds

One important thing to keep in mind if you are buying online is to calculate the shipping fees. You will want to include these costs when you are budgeting expenses and estimating your potential profits.

Another detail to take note of is how many seeds you will be buying. You do not want to end up with an overabundance of seeds that will just go to waste and cut into your profits. On the other hand, you also do not want to short yourself and not have enough seeds to grow the right size crop to meet your expected market demand. The size of your land will help you determine how many seeds you will need to grow a profitable harvest. On average, farmers can expect to pay around 130 dollars in seeds per acre of land.

Seed Varieties

If you do not have much experience growing varieties of plants, then you are going to come across some terms that will be foreign. It is important to understand your seed varieties as this will be detrimental to the production of fruits and vegetables.

Open-pollinated seeds are plants that will pollinate naturally. The wind and insects will ensure that these plants flower and are ready to harvest. These seeds are ideal because you can save seeds from your current crop to plant the next year. Another benefit of these seeds is that the plants tend to adapt better to growing conditions and climate changes each year.

Hybrid or H1 seeds are produced by professional breeders. These seeds are cultivated under controlled pollination methods, not natural pollinators. Many of these seeds are a cross of specific plant varieties that have favorable qualities like being disease-resistant or producing higher-yielding crops. While these seeds will often grow into thriving crops, if you save and reuse the seeds from one season to the next, they will not produce the same plant trait as the original. For this reason, many hybrid seed breeds are not recommended for reuse.

Heirloom seeds refer to the seeds that have been preserved from a parent plant for 40 or more years. These seeds have special genetic diversity and cultural traditions. Many heirloom varieties have distinct appearances, tastes, or characteristics that have allowed them to survive throughout the years.

Organic seeds are derived from plants that have not been exposed to pesticides, fungicides, or synthetic fertilizers. For the purpose of starting a small-scale organic garden, these are the best options. They can be more expensive than other seed varieties but will also ensure that the crops you produce are 100 percent organic.

Genetically modified organism seeds have been altered in labs. These seeds tend to be modified to incorporate specific favorable genes from various plants or to add a more desirable characteristic to an existing plant. GMO seeds are not common, and few are available for small-scale farming, but it is still wise to understand that these seeds do exist. It is more common to find non-GMO seeds.

When purchasing seeds, whether in person or online, you'll want to always check the date on the seeds. The older the date on the package, the less likely they are to germinate. It is best to purchase and use seeds meant for that year of growing.

Tools and Gear

Having the right tools and gear from the beginning of your farming adventure will cut back on time, energy, and stress. You will need a variety of different tools, which will depend on the size and crops your farm will grow.

You will also need a few key hand tools to start your farm. Some you will use as you are working the land others will be essential for building structures, fences, and storage spaces on your land. Tools to consider include:

- Headlamp
- Basic tool kit
- Quality pocket knife
- Electric screwdriver

- Circular saw

- Jigsaw

- Reciprocating saw

- Dump cart

- Spud bar with a tamper end

- Air compressor

- Portable generator

- Ratchet straps

- Tow chain

Garden tools will be your main focus and need.

- Garden hoe

- Scythes

- Sickle

- Shovel (you will want a few different sizes for digging and planting)

- Pitchfork (this is needed for mulching)

- Garden rake

- Triller

- Weed torch (eliminate the need to spray herbicides)

- Soil blocker

- Produce scale

- Garden hose

- Weed whacker, string trimmer, or fence/hedge trimmer

You don't want to work on the farm in any old clothing. For rainy days and cold weather, you will want to have the right clothes to do your farming work in. Some items to have on hand include:

- Muck boots
- Gloves (you will need warm gloves for cold weather, durable gloves for heavy-duty work, and work gloves to keep your hands protected)
- Insulated bib overalls
- Coat
- Moisture-wicking shirts
- Hat
- Sweatband
- Dust mask

One last piece of equipment you will need to invest in for your farming business is a desktop or laptop computer. There are plenty of things you will want a dedicated business laptop for, from tracking weather when you are out in the fields to keeping accounting records and doing marketing work. It will be much easier to track progress, stay organized, and stay on track of your business goals when you have one place to keep all your business-related documents. You do not need to get the best laptop out there, but you do need to get one that will allow you to do everything you need and use it just for your farming business.

Larger Equipment

Aside from the everyday essentials, there are a few larger pieces of equipment you should consider investing in. You will not need everything listed in this section, but you will need some. As your farm grows or you expand your crops, you may want to consider picking up a few other big pieces of machinery. These items will make your farming tasks go faster, and cutting time from these tasks can increase profits. Other items can make the process more efficient, so you can better predict and ensure a hearty harvest.

Tractor

You will need a way to get around your farm, haul tools, transport crops, and move things about from one area to another. Tractors can be a huge investment but are essential for all your farming needs, so you want to choose the right one for your farming needs. When looking to purchase a tractor, keep the following in mind.

- Know how much horsepower the tractor can output. Diesel engine tractors will have more horsepower, and more horsepower means the tractor can handle more intense farming tasks.

- The type of transmission the tractor utilizes is also important. Hydrostatic transmissions are easier to operate, but it is more difficult to maintain a steady speed with them. These transmission tractors require the drive to push on the foot pedals to adjust speed. The harder you push the pedal, the faster it goes. Synchro-shift or manual gear-driven

174

transmission requires you to use a control stick to shift gears. When shifting gears, you need to stop the tractor each time. These types of transmission allow for you to maintain a constant speed but can be more difficult to operate.

- You should know about the power take-off system (PTO). The PTO is positioned in the back of the tractor and powers the attachments used with the tractor. This system will have its own horsepower rating. The higher the horsepower, the more complex the attachments it can handle.

- To use attachments with the tracker, it needs to have a hitch. Tractors can be equipped with different types of hitches. A three-point hitch is designed with a hydraulic lift which can be used with attachments that need to be raised or lowered like a backhoe. A drawbar hitch is used for pulling different attachments. Some drawbar hitches are designed to adjust their center of gravity, even when pulling a load up or downhill. There are also specialized hitches required for front-end loader attachments and forklifts.

- Tractors can also be equipped with hydraulic power-steering systems for easier turning.

- Pay attention to the tires. Most tractor tires have exceptional traction for heavy work, but this requires the tires to be filled with a heavier fluid, not just air. Tires that can be filled with antifreeze fluid for windshield washer fluid will have more weight and better traction. Also, ensure the tractor has a four-wheel drive.

- Know the safety features of the tractor. Almost all tractors have a rollover protective structure that will keep you, or the driver, better protected in case the tractor accidentally flips or rolls.

- Not all tractors will have headlights, but these are essential for earlier farming tasks and late-day projects.

You can get a lot more use out of your tractor when you invest in the right attachment and accessories. These will speed up many farming duties and can save you from having to purchase another large piece of machinery. Some attachments to consider include:

- Cultipackers

- Harrows

- Seed Drills

- Bush hog

- Pallet forks

- Posthole digger

- Box blade

- Backhoe

- Front-end loader

Large full-sized tractors are efficient for a lot of acreages, but if you have a smaller lot of land to farm, consider a subcompact tractor. They are smaller but pack a lot of power and often have a PTO and three-point hitch, making them multi-functional. Another downsized option is a two-wheeled tractor. These tractors work with the driver walking behind the tractor. They can often be used with various attachments though the selection is limited. These units are significantly cheaper than larger, full-sized tractors. You can find a two-wheeled tractor for around 2,000 dollars.

Buying a tractor new will typically cost over 10,000 dollars. Finding a used quality tractor can cost half as much as a new one. This price is without the attachments, each of which can cost a few hundred dollars and up to a few thousand.

Plows

There are many plows you can use on your farm, but not all are the same. The type of plow you need for your farm will depend on the soil and condition of the land. The crops you grow will also influence what plow you use. The most common types of plows include:

- Moldboard- These are large winged plows used to cut and turn over the soil. These should be used if the land you are farming has been untouched or out of production for a while.

- Chisel- Chisel plows will turn over soil about 12 inches deep. These plows are used to incorporate new soil that has been added to the land with older soil that has been used for crop production. This allows for the crop residue left over from the recent harvest to be shifted.

- Disk- A disk plow's purpose is to cut into the soil. This does not turn over the soil like the moldboard or chisel plows.

Most plows can be purchased for 300 dollars.

All-Terrain Vehicles (ATV) or Utility Vehicle (UTV)

ATVs and UTVs are optional but can be useful to haul tools and supplies quickly. If you have a large property that your home sits on and you are using this for your small-scale farm, an ATV or UTV will get you around faster than walking. If a tractor is not within your budget, one of these vehicles can make for a great alternative. While you won't be able to use some of the more intense attachments with an ATV or UTV as you can with a tractor, they pull many of the essentials. Be sure to stick with vehicles that are designed to do more heavy work as opposed to the sporty versions meant for off-roading fun. ATVs and UTVs can be bought for as low as 1,000 dollars, but they can cost up to 10,000 dollars.

Pickup Truck

You can start farming with any type of main vehicle, but a pickup truck is going to be more useful as your farm grows. Trucks will allow you to transport equipment from one location to another and haul all your tools when needed. As you begin to harvest, a pickup truck is going to be invaluable for making local deliveries. Before you trade in your compact car or SUV, you will want to know what you will need your truck for. If you only need it to haul tools from one side of your farm to another, a more sensible option would be a tractor or ATV. However, if you plan on using it for deliveries and setting up a stand at the farmers' market, it can be worth a slight investment.

Always crunch your numbers before you spend. This can be an investment you hold off on until you have a larger customer base where renting a delivery truck or van becomes a greater expense than monthly car payments. If you are mechanically efficient, you can easily find a used truck for a few thousand dollars, but they will often need a significant amount of work. If you can do the work yourself, this can be a budget-friendly option. However, a new truck will cost well over 30,000 dollars.

Wagon or Trailer

A wagon can take on many shapes and sizes. This piece of equipment is attached and pulled by your tractor, ATV, UTV, or truck. Some wagons have two wheels, while others can have four or more. These are essential for hauling various items around the farm or to and from multiple locations. Thes can be purchased for around 200 dollars, but larger, more durable ones can cost over 1,000 dollars. You also have the option to build your own if you are an avid builder or if you just want to put something together for temporary use.

Cultivator

Cultivators will be an essential piece of equipment on your farm. These machines cultivate the soil and prepare the land for planting. They can also be used for weed control when you adjust and properly space the times. Using a cultivator for weed control will require a steady driver as a slight shift to the right or left can take out crops you may have grown already. These machines can be hooked up to a three-point hitch on your tractor. They come in many sizes, and some are designed just for topsoil cultivation, while others are designed for deep soil tilling. If you don't mind the extra effort and do not have a lot of land to cultivate, you can find hand held cultivators that you push from behind to loosen up the soil. Heavy-duty cultivators can cost over 1,000 dollars, while handheld manual cultivators will cost a few hundred dollars.

Cultipacker

These are handy pieces of equipment that will better prepare your soil for planting your seeds. This machine is pulled behind your tractor or ATV to firm the soil and allows leave grooves in the soul to prevent erosion. Once seeds are planted, you can use this to press the seeds into the soil for better contact. Cultipackers can help you maximize your crop production. Smaller ATV size cultipackers will cost around 3oo dollars. Larger cultivators can cost over 1,500 dollars.

Plastic Mulch Layer

Plastic mulch layers are used in plasticulture growing methods, which lay a thin sheet of plastic mulch. An irrigation water system is set up underneath the plastic to supply efficient water to the plants. This method of growing helps with soil temperature control, moisture retention, eliminates weeds, and keeps pests from invading crops. Many farmers can take advantage of this growing method as it also allows for certain crops to be planted ahead of their typical planting seasons, such as strawberries and tomatoes. A plastic mulch layer shapes your planting beds and lays the plastic mulch along the bed.

This is a machine you want to weigh the pros and cons against. Plasticulture growing methods tend to shorten the growing allowing you to harvest much sooner. It can be the right investment, depending on the crops you plan to grow. A larger plastic mulch layer that attaches to your tractor can cost over 2,000 dollars. A smaller walk-behind or low-horsepower tractor attachment will cost a little less than 1,000 dollars. Keep in mind that you do need to have the right water irrigation system in place to work with this planting method which you will need to factor into the overall cost.

Irrigation System

It will be hard to properly water your entire crop using a garden hose, so you'll need a water system in place. Your crops will need consistent water, and some crops will require more than others. Irrigation systems provide a steady and reliable stream of water to the growing field. Irrigation systems can be complex or can be simple do-it-yourself projects. Simple soaker hoses can also be used if you have the ability to connect them to an outdoor spigot. Before you install an irrigation system, you will have to know what crops you will grow and how much watering they will need daily or weekly. Some systems can be set up with multiple tiers or as an even drip system. You want to have a clear understanding of which system will work best for the crops you plan to grow. The most basic systems can be bought for a few hundred dollars.

Advanced irrigation systems that also come equipped with soil moisture sensors can cost well over a thousand dollars. This seems like a pricey investment just to distribute water, but it can have a huge impact on the success of your crops.

Seed Drills

Seed drills will make planting go substantially faster no matter what size farm you start. These machines plant seeds into the ground with little soil disturbances. Crop farms that require rows of seeds to be planted will benefit from these machines. Seed drills can be found as attachments for your tractor and can either be no-till or traditional. No-till drills are designed with blades that cut into the soil and break up leftover crop residue. This will create a clear line for seeds to be planted in. Traditional seed drills do not have blades that cut through the soil, so tilling and plant bed preparation needs to be done separately before planting the seeds. The sole purpose of these types of seed drills is to lay the seeds. Most seed drills will cost at least 1,000 dollars.

If you are in need of a machine that will spread the seeds out over a large area, you'll want to invest in a seeder, also known as a broadcast seeder or rotary spreader. Seed spreaders will help you grow crops and grass. The machine is used to throw out seeds over a large area that does not require the specific placement of seeds. These can be found as small manual handheld spreaders which will cost around 20 dollars. There are also large spreaders that can be attached to your tractor or pulled by your AV, which can cost up to 200 dollars.

Transplanter

A transplanter will make your life easier if you have crops that need to be started indoors or as seedlings before planting into the ground. Those living in colder climates will get a great deal of use out of a transplanter. These machines will dig a hole into the ground and drop the seedling plant into the hole. These machines can be manual pieces of equipment that work by either pressing a lever with your foot or hand to drop the plant. This machine also reduces how much you have to bend over and dig or plant each seedling independently. There are also transplanter attachments that can be pulled by your tractor or ATV. These machines can cost a few thousand dollars, so be sure to honestly consider how much use you will get out of it. If you are planting on a few acres, you might be able to make do with a handheld transplanter, but for farms of ten acres, a tractor-pulled transplanter is essential.

Backhoe

A backhoe is designed with a shovel arm for digging and a bucket for pushing or lifting. A backhoe attachment can be used if your tractor has a hydraulic hitch. Attachment backhoes can dig about ten feet deep. Full-sized backhoe machinery can be a useful piece of equipment if you know you will be doing a lot of digging on your land. For example, if you need to move big boulders out of the way or large clear areas of your land, a backhoe can serve you well. Backhoes can also be helpful when spreading topsoil and fertilizers or when you need to replant trees to other areas of your farm. If you can get multiple uses out of the backhoe, it can be a sensible investment, but for most, renting one may be more suitable for your budget.

There are different sizes of machines you can look into. A mini backhoe can perform many of the farming tasks you need to complete. A standard backhoe is better suited if you need to dig deeper holes greater than ten feet or have more intensive jobs you want to complete with the backhoe. Whether purchasing an attachment for your tractor or buying a mini or standard-sized machine, expect to spend 5,000 dollars for the bucket and shovel attachments and between 10,000 to 30,000 dollars for a mini or standard backhoe.

Front-End Loader

A front-end loader can be a valuable asset for your farm. This machine is equipped with a bucket shovel that you will find many uses for on a daily basis. Like the backhoe, a front-end loader can be found as an attachment for your tractor, or you can find a different size loader. These will allow you to loosen up soil to prepare your land, spread soil, and fertilizer, and can be used to lift and haul heavy equipment.

An attachment piece will cost 2,500 dollars, where a mini or standard front-end loader can cost over 15,000 dollars. So if you are looking for a tractor, find a package deal that includes this equipment, and you can save yourself some money.

Harvester

A harvester is not an essential piece of equipment unless you are planning on harvesting grain. Even if you are only dedicated to a small section of your land for grain, you will need a harvester. A small harvester that you walk behind can cost at least 1,000 dollars. Harvesters that need to be powered by your tractor will cost a few thousand dollars.

Hay Balers and Rakes

Hay balers and rakes are also essential for specific types of farming. For example, those who are planning to produce hay will need a rake to cut the hay and a baler to roll or pack it. There are various types of each to consider, and each can be a heft investment. Combined, you can expect to pay over 10,000 dollars for this equipment. Additionally, hay balers are complex machines with various moving papers that need constant maintenance, which can add up to more than you account for in your budget.

Outsourcing

While it is commendable to take on all the daily tasks required to get your farm up and running, this can cost you in the short and long run. You will want to maintain your excitement for starting your own business, and this will often require delegating tasks to others. Hiring farm workers is not as simple as putting anyone who is looking for a job to work or asking friends or family members to help you out. Some of the duties you might be hiring for are labor-intensive, and the person or people you will hire have to be well aware of their responsibilities. Working the land is not the only place to consider hiring for some extra help. The finances, record keeping, invoicing, marketing, and other aspects that will keep your business operating smoothly are also areas to consider letting someone else take over. Before you start looking for people to work your land, you need to have a clear idea of what tasks you will need to allocate for others to do.

Once you know what positions you need to hire for, it will be good practice to make a short list of ideal qualities, skills, and characteristics of the person or people you want to hire. These might include things like having a good job, excellent communication skills, being able to operate heavy machinery, or bookkeeping. After you list what you are looking for in your hires, you will need to calculate how much you are willing and pay for them to do the desired job descriptions.

You should have a hiring process in mind to ensure that you successfully hire the right people. During your hiring process, you should be conducting interviews to find the right person to work with. Always make it clear to the person you are interviewing what your mission is and what you are trying to achieve. Properly communicating these will help you wean out the bad seeds. Also, consider how much training you can or are willing to provide to the right candidate that shows great enthusiasm but may lack the farming knowledge you initially expected.

Do not sugar coat expectations. You need to hire people who are going to put in full effort every day. People will not give their full effort if they are led to believe that the tasks they would be doing are easy when really, they might even go without sleep, be sore from manual labor, and have to be adaptable. Set clear expectations from the very beginning, and those not fully committed will take themselves out of the pool of prospects. It is easy to weed out the people who will not be a good fit on the farm, but it can take a little creative thinking. Those who really want the job and are excited about getting their hands dirty to accomplish the business goals you have already stated will go the extra mile to stand out.

Consider hiring on a trial period. It is not uncommon to hire someone who says all the right things during an interview and looks good on paper only to have them come to work and be completely disappointed. There are many reasons why someone may not be a good fit for your business, and it is better to let them go sooner rather than later. Let those applying for the position know that they will be hired for a trial period, for about one month, three months, six months, and at which point you will evaluate the work they have done and sit down with them to review their position.

Avoid hiring a jack of all trades. While you want to minimize your cost when hiring, you do not want to cut corners. Each person you hire should have specific duties; one person minds the water system, the other operates the planter, and everyone should know what they need to be doing. If there is any confusion, they can contact you to resolve issues.

Although farming is taxing work, you need to keep the environment upbeat and enjoyable. Otherwise, you won't have people enthusiastic about coming in for the day. Find ways to show the people you hire that you appreciate their hard work. These people can be a great asset in helping you make changes to get your business operation running more smoothly. They are the ones that can come to you with suggestions for how to streamline production, cut costs, or spot issues that hinder the growth of your crops. If they feel like they are only going to be belittled or yelled at, they are not going to come to you with solutions. Your employees will be more productive and satisfied with the work they do on your farm if you encourage them to take ownership of what they do and listen to their ideas.

What happens when you hire the wrong person? The wrong help can cost you money, time, and even your reputation. You need to address the issues as quickly as possible and either let them go or reiterate the expectation established during the interview and then let them go.

Crafting the Right Business Plan

Though not something you need to purchase, a business plan is essential for getting started. Many people neglect to take the time to create a proper business plan, and this is why many small businesses fail to succeed or grow to their fullest potential. A business plan should be a detailed document that clearly maps out the life of your farming business. It will serve as a roadmap to follow for many aspects of your business. Before you go looking for funding, mapping out how to use your land, or purchasing any gear, create a business plan. You will need a plan to keep you focused and aligned with why you are starting this journey.

Business plans are essential for staying aligned and focused on your short and long-term business goals. To gain funding, most lenders will request a review of your business plan, and this will be a huge determining factor as to whether or not you get a loan, grants, or other types of funding for your small farm. Therefore, before you begin obtaining tools, equipment, or asking for money, you need to write a business plan. Your business plan will help guide you to what you want to accomplish with your farming business and gives you the appropriate time to work through your goals without wasting money or making unnecessary investments before you get started.

While these plans can vary in length, yours should include:

- Your business farm objectives
- Farming activities such as products or services your farm will provide
- Short and long term goals
- Estimated cost for doing business
- Expected risks or obstacles your business will face and how to overcome them
- An action plan to achieve goals
- An executive summary
- A marketing strategy
- Market research and analysis
- A description of your target market
- Knowledge of the biggest competition in your market
- Financial plan
- Clear monthly, quarterly, and annual budget breakdown
- Project growth or expansion goals

When writing a business plan, you will want to include as much detail as possible without the document becoming overly complex. Someone reading it should gain a clear understanding of the type of business you are starting, the products you will provide, the basic operations, project growth, and how you will accomplish the financial goals established. Expect your business plan to be between 15 to 20 pages long.

Your business plan will help get your business started and should be reviewed at least annually to ensure you are on track with your business goals. This document is not set in stone. You can and should update as your business grows or you decide to take your business in a new direction. It is advisable to review your business plan as a way to look at what you have accomplished, what hasn't been achieved, goals you may have lost focus on, and as motivation to continue with your small-farm business.

Drafting a Small Farm Business Plan

This section will give you a better idea of how to organize and write a successful business plan for your small farm. Your business plan will be divided into sections that will include all the information mentioned previously. Your business plan will be unique and original to your values, goals, and codes of conduct. The front page of your business plan should clearly display your business name, logo, address, contact information, and a brief line that defines your business. After the front page, you should have a table of contents that lists page numbers for the executive summary, products and services, market analysis, marketing strategy, financial planning, budget, and other considerations. We will go into further detail about what each of these sections should include below. If you have applications for permits, these should be noted in the main body of the business plan and then included as appendices once the plan is completed.

Executive Summary

The executive summary is the first thing lenders will read when they review your business plan. The most important component of the executive summary is the mission statement. This statement is a short and concise paragraph that defines your business purpose. The mission statement takes into consideration the goals, values, and objectives of your business. When written correctly, the mission statement is what you will refer to when making a big decision about your farming business and will establish expectations for how the business should be run, the work culture. The big picture goals everyone involved is working towards.

Your mission statement should summarize what your business does, how it does it, and why it does what it is doing. This statement alone will tell investors if your business values and goals align with their own values and whether or not they want to invest in your business. It is also recommended that you add a vision statement after your mission statement. The vision statement takes the mission statement into consideration to establish a long-term goal you wish to accomplish through your business.

For example, Nike's mission statement is: "Create groundbreaking sports innovations, make products sustainably, build a creative and diverse global team, and make a positive impact in communities where we live and work" (Law, 2021). In addition, the company's vision statement is: "Bring inspiration and innovation to every athlete in the world. If you have a body, you are an athlete" (Law, 2021).

You can keep these two statements separate as their own section or combine them into a mission and vision statement section in your executive summary. While these statements are a crucial component, it is not something many businesses perfect on the first draft. It can take a few years to write a mission statement that clearly establishes your business goals and values. This statement is something you will often revisit and make adjustments to as you can gain more business experience and evaluate what is most important to you and your business operations.

If you are struggling to come up with a concise mission statement, move on to writing out the short and long-term goals for your business. Your goals should expand into five years or your business life. Use the SMART goal method to create goals that are specific, measurable, achievable, relevant, and time-sensitive. With this approach, you will be able to map out big and small wins for your business that will propel you towards a profitable and successful business.

The executive summary will also include main details about your farming business such as partners, owners or business leaders, employees, business operations, how many acres your farm is, and where it is located. You can include background information in this section to give readers a better idea of who you are. Tell them how long you have been farming or your history with farming. What type of farming techniques are you familiar with and plan to use for growing and harvesting? What environmental impact are you hoping to make with your small farm?

Products and Services

This section will do more than list the products or services your small farm will provide. The products and services section will also provide pricing, product lifespan predictions, production and manufacturing processes, and how customers benefit from the products supplied. This is also the section where patents acquired will be mentioned.

If you have any research and development information, you will outline it in this section as well. This section should give you and lenders the profit potentials of your small farm.

Market Analysis

The marketing sections are where you may spend more time researching and gathering more information. You can not expect your farm to do well if you do not have the cognizance of your target market and the farming industry. Market analysis will include information on competitors, their strengths and weaknesses, and details about customer demand. The best way to organize this section is with SWOT analysis; strengths, weaknesses, opportunities, and threats. With this analysis, you look at external and internal factors that can benefit or hinder your farming business. You will need to take into consideration various farming information and list the advantages and disadvantages of using one method over another. Here, you will list any struggles or risks your business will encounter as well as systems or ideas that can benefit your farm's entrance into the market.

Marketing Strategy

The marketing strategy will cover all the steps you plan to take to get your products in front of customers. You will need to describe what customers will learn about your business, how to establish a loyal customer base, and how to reach a larger audience. You will need to know what platform you will use for your advertising, customer attraction, and retention, such as advertisements, social media, and word of mouth. The more details and steps provided in the marketing strategy, the more success you will have with your marketing plan. In this section, you'll also want to decide how much money you will allocate for marketing and how exactly it will be used.

Financial Planning

The financial planning sections are what lenders will review thoroughly. This section should include all financial statements and balance sheets. As a new business, you won't have accurate accounts for most of this information. Instead, most of the documents here will be estimates or target price points for the first three years of your business. Also, be sure to mention potential investors in this section.

An important sub-section to include in the financial planning portion are the financial projections. They will be titled as pro formas and based on future financial expectations. Here, you will include the overall budget, not including one-time expenses. These documents are based on current market conditions and used to create a hypothetical outlook for revenues and money flow. These will also include expected market changes that will influence your business' potential to earn.

Budget

Creating a budget is one of the first things you need to do when starting a business, so this section should be fairly easy and quick to complete. The budget section of your business plan will list all the costs of running and maintaining your business which include daily expenses, wages, supplies, insurance, and marketing. You'll want to create a budget for your expected monthly expenses and include a budget for quarterly or annual expenses. Having a precise budget will help you uncover your true cost of business and may lead to having to make cuts to reduce spending until your farm is better established.

Other Considerations

This last component of the business plan is optional but can be used to get a better, more defined picture of the potential you see for your farm. Other considerations can include additional drawbacks or concerns about running a small-scale farm. In addition, you can include modifications to systems or processes being implemented and highlight innovative techniques that are growing your business. This section is to provide you, partners, and lenders any additional and interesting facts or ideas you have about the growth of your business.

Chapter 4:
Organize the Legal Side

If you are still committed to moving forward with your farming goals, there are some key things you'll need to carefully consider first. The most important factor is funding your farm. You have just read about some of the things you will need just to get your farm started, and this may have gotten you thinking that there is no way you can pursue this type of business. There are many ways you can get funding for your farm to cover startup costs as well as to expand in the future. Knowing your options will help you feel more confident about starting your farm without having to go into serious debt.

Starting your own farming business also means there are certain legal steps you need to take to keep you and your farm protected. These are not things you want to delay taking care of because neglecting to obtain the right documents can result in not being able to sell your produce for a profit, and this can lead to huge losses.

Do You Have Enough Funds?

As we covered in the first chapter, going into debt is not any part of the process. You will want to ensure that before you begin, you have enough money to begin cultivating and developing your crops. If you do not, you might want to postpone or have another option for obtaining the money to get started. Some ways you can secure funds for starting your farm are discussed below.

Grants

Grans are the best option for getting money to cover the upfront cost of starting your small farm. Unlike other funding, you do not have to worry about repaying grant money.

There are a variety of grants available for small to mid-sized farmers, especially if you will also be provided an educational element such as teaching the community about growing food. The Specialty Crop Block Grant Program provides funding to farmers growing fruits, vegetables, nuts, and nursery plants that will be used by people. The crops can be used for food, medical purposes, or for aesthetics. These include a wide range of crops like grapes, olives, strawberries, and tomatoes. You can find a full list of eligible plants on the United States Department of Agriculture. This is a highly competitive grant, and not all states participate in the programs. It is advisable you review the information provided by the USDA website about the Specialty Crop Block Grant Program.

Additional grant programs to be aware of:

- Farmers Market Promotion Program
- Local Food Promotion Program
- Federal-State Marketing Improvement Program
- Acer Access and Development Program
- Specialty Crop Multi-State Program
- Regional Food System Partnerships

There are also additional grants available for those raising livestock on their farm. This is good to keep in mind if you plan on expanding or including sheep, cows, or chickens on your farms as well.

You will also find an extensive list of available grants on the USDA National Institute of Food and Agricultures Site. This will list what type of farm they are available for, how much funding is provided, and other details about eligibility. Additional resources to look into for grant and loan opportunities include:

- The National Sustainable Agriculture Coalition's Guide to USDA Funding for Local and Regional Food Systems
- Natural Resources Conservation Service
- The Conversation Stewardship Program
- The National Sustainable Agriculture Information Service (ATTRA)
- USDA National Agricultural Library General Funding Resource Page
- USDA Sustainable Agriculture Research and Education Program
- National Institute of Food and Agriculture Beginning Farmer and Rancher Development Program
- The Clif Bar Family Foundation

You can also look for additional funding opportunities available in your state on the National Council of State Agricultural Finance Program. If you notice your state is not listed for additional grants or loans, reach out to your State's Department of Agriculture office to learn what options are available for you.

Before you begin applying to grant programs, you need to have a well-written business plan. Most grant applications will require a document describing your farm. You will want to include information about your farm operations, the number of employees you plan to hire and their job descriptions, estimated salary for employees, operation cost, and expected revenue. Your business plan should also include an executive summary, goals, partners involved, a timeline for your farming operations, short and long-term costs, and an estimated budget.

If approved for a grant, it is imperative that you document how you have spent the money and keep records of how the money has helped you reach your farming goals. It is possible that additional funding opportunities will be provided to help you maintain your farm and future advance in your goals.

If writing a grant application is overwhelming or you do not feel you can do an adequate job of writing a grant proposal, you can hire a professional grant writer. A professional will know how to write a successful application. They may also be able to provide you information or find additional grants to apply to, or find a more secure fund for your agriculture business. Those living in the midwest of the United States can take advantage of free grant advising through the Michael Funds Agricultural Institute. Other useful resources to help with grant funding include:

- Center for Rural Affairs Farm Finances Page

- Government Grants for Small Businesses (a farm is considered a small business)

- National Council of State Agricultural Finance Programs Aggie Bonds for Beginning Farmers

- The Farmer's Guide to Agricultural Credit

- The Center for Farm Financial Management

- The Carrot Project (non-for-profit that provides resources to small and mid-sized farmers)

Loans

Loans may be easier to obtain than grants and can often provide you with more funding. Obtaining a loan is dependent on your credit score and experience. These loans can be used for:

- Purchasing land
- Operating expenses
- Marketing
- Farm equipment
- Expanding operations

There are several places you can turn to for a variety of loan services for agriculture businesses. These include:

- Local banks
- Farm Service Agency (FSA)
- Housing and Community facility Program (for purchasing land)
- Farm Credit Services

You can search the National Council of State Agricultural Finance Programs website to find a list of loan programs available in your state.

To increase your approval chances, you'll want to ensure you are on good credit. Each loan opportunity will have a set of requirements to meet, and your credit score will be a huge determining factor. A credit score of 660 or above will typically put you in good credit standing.

You will also need to have your business plan available for review. The lender will want to know what they are investing in, so it is important to have a well-organized and compelling business plan.

Know the type of loan you will need. There are several different types of agricultural loans you can apply for, and each will have guidelines or requirements you must meet before approval. You need to know what these requirements are and ensure that your farm is eligible. There are also emergency loans for those who have a farm in a disaster counter or for farmers who have suffered from a 30 percent or more loss due to unfortunate circumstances.

Increase Your Loan Acceptance

Despite there being plenty of loan opportunities for farmers and small business owners, it's very difficult to apply or access funds if you do not have proof to show your profits. However, if you are just getting started with small-scale farming, you should be able to answer a few key questions to get financing for your farm.

1. What size farm do you need to reach your financial goals?

2. Will you be operating in a small or large market?

3. Do you need to purchase land or facilities to start your farm?

4. Is there a demand for the crops you intend on growing?

5. Do you have a marketing plan? What does it look like?

6. Will you diversify your crops?

Aside from being able to answer these questions, it is crucial to have your own personal finances in order. When you are just getting started, you may have to rely on your own savings to acquire a few customers. Gaining these customers will give you some proof that your small farm has the potential to become profitable. Keep exceptional records of your business operations as you grow your customer list.

When you are ready to apply for a loan, have the following documents ready for the lender to review.

- Know how much you are going to be requesting and create a breakdown of how you will use the funds.

- Have balance sheets that show your assets, the money you are waiting to receive, and any outstanding debts you need to pay.

- Include an income statement that covers your profits and losses for the past year.

- Provide lenders with a state of cash flow.

- You will need to have proof of insurance.

- A marketing plan that details how you are going to gain customers and get your product to the customers.

- You will need to show your credit history.

What If You Have Bad Credit?

While it is not easy, it is still possible to get a loan when you do not meet the recommended credit score. If you have a low credit score, there are a few steps you can take to get funding for your business.

1. Look for low-credit lenders. These lenders will offer loan services, but there will be a much higher interest rate for the loan. It is important that if you choose a low-credit lender that you work to improve your credit score. Once you have a better score, you can always refinance your loan, so you get a lower interest rate.

2. Have proof of your faring experiences. Government lending programs tend to be more concerned about your farming history than with your credit score. You will need to have an impressive farming history to prove you are fit to start and operate a successful farm to be approved for a government loan, even if your credit score is subpar.

3. Find a co-signer. If you can find a co-signer that has better credit than you, you are more likely to get approved for an agricultural loan.

4. Apply for income-based loans. Loan providers may have income-based loans available. These will vary but will often have a minimum income requirement. Many farmers find they can get approved for these types of loans faster though they are often not as much as other funding options.

Seed Money and Angel Investors

There is also the option to obtain seed money or find angel investors. Seed funding is usually a small amount of money that helps cover the most basic startup cost and gives your capital a boost. This funding can lead to larger funding opportunities if you can show a track record of profitability. Seed money can be obtained through crowdfunding, large companies or corporations, incubators, accelerators, venture capitalists, and angel investors.

Angel investors can be a single individual or small group of individuals willing to help companies or startups develop their business idea. They typically have an in-depth understanding of farm operations and the industry so they can be able to best gauge the success or failure of a particular person looking for funding. These lenders can include large companies, incubators, accelerators, and venture capitalists. They will offer small lending opportunities for startups at different cycles of its growth.

You will need to have a long-term plan for angel investors to consider. The more your farm grows and reaches the financial goals you have established, the more likely the angel investor will want to be a part of your success.

Do You Have the Land?

Purchasing land is a huge investment and is the most important component for the success of your business. If you already have land, then you are well on your way to starting your own farm. If you do not have land, you need to look into obtaining some acreage to get you started, and this may require you to take out a loan to make the purchase. You can also find people who are willing to rent their land to you. You will be surprised by how many people have acres upon acres of land that are just sitting unused. These people may be willing to rent the land to you to start farming in exchange for a portion of the profits. This can be a great way to find land to start on without having to pay a huge upfront cost or worry about loan repayments. The downside to this is that you do not own the land. At any point, the person who does own the land can change what you initially agree upon or sell the property leaving you with nothing to work on. This can be especially devastating if you have put a year or more of hard work into the land.

Carefully weigh the pros and cons before you make this buying decision. Having your own land does mean greater independence and security, but it also means much greater debt.

Licenses and Permits

When purchasing land, you will want to ensure that it is permitted and ready for farming. If it is not, you will have to obtain the right documents to begin farming for profit. This is also something you need to do if you already have land that you will be working on. There are certain restrictions imposed on farms that will not allow you to sell what you harvest unless you have the right legal documents to do so.

You will need to obtain the right licenses and permits to operate your small-scale farm. These can vary from state to state and be dependent on specific locations, and you will need to obtain these from both the state and federal levels.

The types of permits and licenses required will depend on your business activity and government rules. These will also impact the fees you need to pay to obtain these documents.

The U.S. Department of Agriculture makes it easy to apply for agriculture permits. Two permits you need to consider to obtain are Plant Health Permits and Protected Plant Permits.

Do You Need Insurance?

Your agriculture business, just like any business, will need to be properly insured. Farm insurance will protect you from the many legal issues that you will encounter during the development, growth, and lifespan of your farm. Aside from protection against injury, property damage, and product liability claims, having insurance can help you regain and recover losses due to extreme weather, pest problems, and other disasters that are out of your control. Getting the right coverage will take some research. This is not something you just want to rush through making a decision on. Below are some key factors to understand when insuring your farm.

- A standard homeowner's policy is not sufficient to cover your farming business. If you are just farming for yourself, this could be enough to protect your land but will often not cover farming equipment or machinery. For a farming business, you need to look at different policies.

- Hobby farm insurance can be obtained for those who plan to sell their produce at local farmers' markets. A hobby farm is not bigger than 500 acres wide and only has one location. Hobby farms cannot generate more than 10,000 dollars a year and cannot have staff or employees.

- You will want to consider a farm owner's insurance policy. These policies are for higher-profit generating farms, and there are many aspects of the policy that can be modified to suit your farm's needs. With farm owner's insurance, your farm is treated as a full-time place of employment and will include things like liability coverage and loss prevention.

- Do not go with a standard farm insurance policy. This is a big mistake many beginners make. They find a bundle policy that uses fixed coverage across all areas of their business. Your farm is unique, and you need to get a policy that is customized to your farm's risks and needs.

- Ensure that any structure or building on your farm is covered. Some policies will consider buildings used for farming operations (sheds, silos, or barns) as commercial buildings, and certain policies will not cover these structures.

- Know the details of what invalidates the policy. For example, it is a good idea to have fire protection included in your insurance policy, but many factors can contribute to you not being fully covered. You need to know how far hydrants or access to water needs to be in relation to buildings and fields. Covering your machinery and farm equipment is also highly recommended, but this has special guidelines for properly maintaining the equipment or risk loss of coverage if the machine needs to be repaired or replaced.

- Try to negotiate in getting the fencing on your farm included in the polity. Most policies do not cover fencing, and your farm is going to have various fences which will need regular maintenance and repairs. Getting the fencing cover can save you in the long term, but this comes at a higher premium.

- If you plan on raising livestock on your farm, you will need an additional insurance policy. Farm liability insurance will not cover damage or injury from livestock.

- Custom farming, where you are not actively involved in the dairy farming activities and instead pay someone else to operate the farm, requires a different insurance policy.

- Vehicle coverage like your tractor, ATV, UTV, or farm truck will not be covered under farm insurance. These will require you to obtain additional auto coverage, and some state it is mandatory to have these vehicles properly insured.

- If you are employing individuals to work on your farm, you need to have proper workers' compensation. The requirements vary by state. Some states make it mandatory that you have workers' compensation if the combined salary of your workers meet a minimum. Other states want you to have a policy that will protect workers from injuries obtained while on the job. Even if it is not mandatory for you to have a workers' compensation policy in effect, it is still a good choice to have one.

Blanket vs. Individual Coverage

Two of the most common coverages you can choose from are blanket coverage or individual coverage. Blanket coverage, also referred to as unscheduled, covers all of your farm's property, including structures on the land, equipment, and livestock. This coverage lets you pay one lump sum depending on the sum of all your assets. When agreeing on this coverage, you need to have accurate calculations of your asset. Not having the correct value of your assets can lead to being underinsured, and you will not be able to make a claim due to loss.

Individual coverage, also referred to as scheduled coverage, lets you choose what assets you want to be covered and decide on an amount to be insured. This type of coverage can be better as it will allow you to prioritize assets that are of higher value.

Crop Insurance

While farm insurance policy covers a majority of your farm operation liabilities, this doesn't protect your crops. Instead, you will need Multiple Peril Crop insurance or Crop-Hail Insurance. Multiple Peril Crop insurance is government-funded insurance, though you can obtain this insurance from private providers, rates and premiums are established by the Federal Crop Insurance Corporation (FCIC). This insurance covers most natural disaster losses like those from drought or crop disease. This insurance, however, will not cover all types of crops. Crops that are covered include:

- Cotton
- Corn
- Wheat
- Soybeans

It is possible to ask for your specific crops to be covered if they are considered less common in your specific locations. It is vital that you ask if all your crops will be covered. Otherwise, you can suffer great losses.

Crop-Hail Insurance can be obtained from a private insurance provider. Coverage is obtained based on the acres you want to insure. You do not have to insure your entire farm. With this insurance, your crops will be protected against specific events such as damage from weather conditions like hail, extreme wind, and lightning. You may also be able to get fire protection with this policy. Unfortunately, you can not get protection from frost, drought, or excessive rain/moisture. Your farm's location will impact what you can get covered, so it is best to do thorough research on what is and is not included based on your location. You can obtain this insurance at any time of your growing season.

You can obtain both Multiple Peril insurance and Crop-Hail insurance to better protect your crops.

Chapter 5:
Know Your Seeds and What They'll Become

Now that you understand the beginning steps, it is time to start moving your dream of having a successful farm into a reality. Farms can be of many varieties. Will you be a vegetable farmer, grow only herbs, or have a botanical garden? Knowing what you want to grow is the first step to planning out a successful business. You do not want to be passive about this and think it will be nice to have a field of corn or an apple orchard. You'll want to be specific and clear about the type of farm you will have. This will have an impact on your potential profits as well as the other essentials you will need to get started growing.

Choosing the Right Farm

A small farm is typically less than 180 acres, and to be successful, you will not need that much land. You can make even a small section of land work for you and your goals to become a successful farmer. What will get you to that success is a well thought out plan for the short-term so that you can begin making a profit that will lead you to the long term.

Before committing to the type of farm you want to begin, review your profit margins. Some plants will produce crops quickly. Others, like fruit orchards, will take a year before they produce a crop, and even then, there is no guarantee they will produce mature fruits. You can absolutely add these types of crops into your profit margin, but understand that this will be a long-term investment with no short-term gains.

Types of Farms

Small farms can take on many forms. The most common types of farms include:

- Subsistence farms, which produce just enough food to provide for a single-family. These farms typically do not produce a surplus of produce, so there is nothing to sell for profits. Although there is no income, this type of farm can be ideal for those still unsure if they want to dive into a profitable farm venture.

- Commercial farms include any type of farm that raises or grows foods for profit, such as fish farms, dairy farms, or meat farms. Commercial farms can be the primary source of income for individuals.

- Crop farms can be a type of commercial farm but focus on growing fruits, vegetables, or grains. You can have a small crop farm that only grows one type of plant or that grows a selection of plants for profit. They can also grow different varieties of the same type of plant.

- Herb garden farms focus on growing herbs and spice plants. A herb garden can be a great addition to crop farms as many herbs can grow fast and plentiful.

- Bee farms are farms for those who want to sell bee products such as beeswax, pollen, and honey. These farms have a lower start-up cost, which makes them favorable for beginners.

- Microgreen farms are surprisingly a high-demand type of farm. Microgreens are baby plants, usually 14 days old, and have a maximum height of three feet. These plants are used for garnishes and salads in many restaurants.

- Hydroponics farms grow crops in nutrient water as opposed to in the group. These farms are favored by those who want to minimize water waste and pollution that other types of farms can cause. Since you do not need to plant in the ground, you do not need a lot of acres for a hydroponics farm. Most of these farms use a wall design to grow the plants on. These farms do require more management and can be most costly to start because you have to set up the right hydroponics systems.

- Tea gardens or farms specialize in growing plants to use for tea products. Those living in city space who want to give farming a try may achieve their dreams by having a rooftop tea garden. You will want to review building code regulations and restrictions before you start a rooftop garden.

- Mushroom farms grow a variety of mushrooms that can be grown outdoors or indoors in a better-controlled environment. Beginners may like this idea as mushrooms can be easy to grow and are typically ready for harvest in six weeks. Learning how to grow specialty mushrooms like oyster mushrooms can be more profitable as these tend to be in higher demand.

- Organic farms are usually crop farms but can also include livestock farms. These farms focus on natural and organic growing methods.

- Flower farms grow various flooring plants. This type of farm can lead to multiple and easy-to-implement diversifying opportunities. These farms can offer garden tours, supply products to local flower shops, and even work with large venues to create flower arrangements for special events.

- Fruit picking farms are farms that allow visitors to pick their own fruits. This type of farm has many benefits. You can create two different streams of income from one crop, you can harvest some of the crops yourself and sell them around your community, and you generate an income by allowing people to come and purchase what they pick themselves. By having people come to you, these farms also have lower transportation costs.

Profitable Crops to Consider

Herbs- Herbs do not require a large space, so if you only have an acre or so, herbs can be a profitable choice. These plants tend to remain fairly small and are easy to manage. You can sell the herbs as a fresh bundle or dry them and sell them in small spice bottles. You can also have a nice selection of herbs sold in pots that people can buy and place on their countertops. You can even expand on this further by finding creative ways for people to purchase indoor herb walls or mini herb gardens, and this can be done without costing you more time.

Bamboo- Bamboo has many uses, making it a high-demand crop. An acre of bamboo can potentially earn you 25,000 dollars. What makes this a profitable crop is that bamboo does not require as much care or attention to grow in abundance. They can also be grown year-round and typically regrow annually. Those who want a crop that is beneficial for the environment should consider bamboo. While this crop is profitable once it gets growing, bamboo does tend to have higher start-up costs. A single plant can cost 35 dollars, and you will need quite a few to cover an acre to see a return on your investment.

Lavender- This flowering plant is a profitable choice because it can be sold in various ways. Lavender plants can be sold as-is. They can also be processed, and the oil can be sold, or they can be dried and sold as loose leaf tea. Selling lavender oil can bring in a revenue of 27,000 dollars, and this can be accomplished with just an acre of lavender plants. However, if you plan to process the plants yourself, you will need to consider how to properly extract the oil from the plant, and this can add up to more cost and time.

Garlic- Garlic is always in high demand, and garlic crops are fairly easy to maintain. They are also cold weather crops. You can plant them in the fall and harvest them at the beginning of summer. The upfront cost of getting a garlic crop started can be more expensive than other crops, but an acre can generate an income of 100,000 dollars. When you subtract the start-up cost, you are still left with over 80,00 dollars in profits.

Microgreens- Microgreens have a fast turnaround time and are easy to grow, and you do not need a lot of acres to grow a profitable crop. These plants can be grown indoors, so you can easily have a year-round source of income. The only downside is that your market is primarily restaurants, but with the right market plan, you may be able to appeal to other customers. You can expect to garnish 50 dollars per pound sold.

Seasonal Crops

To get the most out of your farm, you need to take your location into careful consideration. Many crops will grow seasonally. Knowing which plants to grow for their ideal season will ensure you always have something to produce and bring in a profit year-round.

Understand how to read a planting calendar. A planting calendar will help you determine what crops to grow and when for the best harvest. Timing your planting is essential. For example, planting seeds that favor warm weather too early before the last frost will destroy your crop. On the other hand, planting seeds too late in the season can result in a loss of crops too, as they may not produce a crop before the weather changes again. Planting calendars simplify the planting process by dividing areas into zones and provide the best month to plant-based on the zone your farm falls into.

Most plants will be planted based on the first and last frost dates of your zone. However, after or before these dates, you can begin to understand how to stagger your crops, so you will have something to harvest throughout the entire season.

Before You Start Planting

Before you start digging up your land, there are some essential things to keep in mind. To ensure you can begin planting as quickly as possible, be sure to have everything in order first.

Seeds vs. Starter Plants

There are pros and cons to starting crops from seeds or starter plants. Each of these planting methods will require transplanting your crop into your fields or farming bed.

Starting with seeds will give you a much wider selection of plants to choose from. Buying seeds from an online catalogue will also allow you to try unique seeds that you won't find at your local nursery.

Seeds are also ideal when you are planting a large number of plants to harvest. You can save hundreds of dollars growing your crops from seeds as opposed to buying all these plants as starters.

Starting slow-growing plants from seeds indoors, early in the season, will ensure they are ready for transplant and should be ready to harvest not much long after planting in the ground. In addition, having seeds to start during the typical non-growing season will give you something to keep you busy. It can also be much more satisfying knowing that you have been caring for your crops from the very beginning. However, waiting to start long-season plants until the recommended seeding time can result in waiting much longer before the plants are ready to harvest, which can have a negative impact on your profits.

While seeds can be the best choice for beginners as purchasing the seeds can be the most cost-efficient, this does not always mean you are going to save money. To start crops from seeds, you will often start them indoors. This usually means you need a dedicated greenhouse or structure on your farm for seedlings. Depending on where you are located, you will need to invest in growing lights to ensure the seedlings are getting adequate light. Despite these upfront investments, there are usually just one-time expenses. Buying seeds each year can save hundreds of dollars every season.

Starter plants can also be beneficial because they are quick and easy to plant. You won't have to wait around for your seedling to reach a certain height or be disappointed if the seeds do not sprout. Starter plants are convenient for those who are juggling a busy schedule while trying to get their farm started.

You do not have to worry about finding the right space to keep your plants. You will be planting these right into your fields, so there is no need for an indoor space or worry about them getting enough light to flourish.

Starter plants have already progressed through the most fragile growing process. Seeds are susceptible to many diseases that will kill them off before it breaks through the soil. However, starter plants have already survived through the uncertainties and are ready to thrive in the ground.

Starter plants will require less care and maintenance. Seeds need to be hardened off, move outdoors, and after eight weeks are then ready to be planted in the ground. Starter plants will not require this extra time before you can anticipate them being ready for planting. In addition, once starter plants are in the ground, you typically do not have to wait as long as you would with seedlings before seeing your first flowering signs of fruit or vegetable growth.

If anything holds up your planning process, such as not getting the beds ready on time or a sudden late frost, you can easily push back your planting schedule. Using starter plants can get you back on your growing schedule. Since starter plants take less time until they are ready to harvest, you can actually end up ahead of schedule. This is not something you always want to do on purpose, though.

With some crops, you want to avoid both seedling and stater plant options. For example, root crops like carrots, beets, and radish fare much better when the seeds are sowed directly into the ground. Other plants that do better when started in the ground include:

- Leafy greens
- Beans
- Cucumbers
- Garlic
- Corn
- Peas

- Pumpkins

- Squash

- Okra

- Watermelon

- Eggplant

- Zucchini

- Brussels sprouts

- Cabbage

- Celery

- Poppies

There are also plants that are not grown from seeds but instead are started from root division or bulbs. These plants include:

- Artichoke

- Asparagus

- Onions

- Potatoes

- Sweet potatoes

- Rhubarb

While it is your choice whether you start from seeds or starter plants, this is a choice you need to make way ahead of planting season. Have a plan outlined for how you will get your crops started and a strategy ready to get them in the ground so that you get to harvesting successfully.

Planting Techniques

Planting techniques vary from farmer to farmer and are often established through a lot of trial and error and experimentation. Each farm will yield different results when harvest time arrives due to a number of variables. Planting date, tilling practice, pests, and plant performance will all have an impact on crop growth and success, and all of these can be different from one farm to the next. You can come up with your own solid planting techniques by first getting advice from other farmers. Knowing what works and does not work with them will supply you with options. Remember, just because something does not work for them does not mean it can't work for you.

Suppose you do not have much experience yet in growing a larger crop. In that case, it is best to follow established recommendations for when to plant, what depth to plant, soil condition, and other factors that, on average, lead to healthy plant growth and germination. Once you have a grasp of what to do successfully, you can begin making adjustments to a few factors that can lead to a higher yield at harvest time. You may find that you can start your seeds a week or two earlier than recommended with no impact on harvest, except that you can harvest a little earlier. Some crops you will learn will do better being planted at a slightly deeper depth than recommended based on soil conditions and produce a better yield at harvesting. When making changes to how you plant, only doing this will be a small percent of your total crops. This will minimize your risk of losing your entire crop if the changes you make are unsuccessful. Keep track of these planting details and their results during your growing season so you can find the best times and techniques for planting.

Seed Placement

There is a reason why you see stretches of farmland laid out in seemingly perfect precise rows. When you properly place your seeds or start plants in a uniform manner, you are more likely to see a more uniform harvestable crop. Seeds need to be planted at the same depth if you want your crop to emerge at the same time. A planter can help you achieve uniformity and boost your productivity and efficiency.

When planting, placing the seeds at the right depth can make a huge difference in when seeds emerge and how much your crop produces. Seeds need enough moisture to begin the growth process. They also need a warm environment to grow in. If you plant your seeds too shallow, the soil can dry quickly and slow down the growing process. On the other hand, planting too deep and the soil temperature can be too cold, and you will not see a great yield when harvesting. Soil conditions will change from one growing season to the next, so it is important to know when you may need to plant a little deeper to ensure the seed receives enough moisture and when to plant a little shallow to ensure the seeds have enough warmth.

One final factor to be mindful of when placing seeds is referred to as closing the trench. Closing the trench means you properly place soil on top of the seed so that there is no air gap between the soil and seed. If not closed properly, this air gap will prevent moisture from reaching the seed. You need to ensure that you cover seeds adequately and then press the topsoil slightly to achieve seed-to-soil contact.

Caring For Your Crops

No matter what type of crop you plant, all will require the same three key factors for proper growth. These are water, sunlight, and nutrient-rich soil. Not all plants require the same amount of these three items. For example, some plants need a lot of water, while some grow much better in the shade. As you gain more experience growing and harvesting your crops, you will begin to learn how to provide each crop the right mixture of these components. Two things that will hinder plant growth despite getting adequate water, sun, and nutrients are pests and weeds.

Pest Problems

One of the biggest and most disruptive issues you will encounter as a farmer will be pests. Pest can include bugs, insects, rodents, deer, and birds who will feast on your crops. You need to take the necessary precautionary measures to keep your crops protected from the various pests that will destroy them. Fencing needs to be put up around the perimeter of the crop areas to keep bigger pests away, like deer. Using covers over the crops can help deter birds from swooping in and picking foods off the plants.

Insect and other bugs are more complex issues. You do not want to use harsh chemicals on your plants to keep these pests away. Anything you spray on your crops will get absorbed into the edible parts of the plant, which will then be consumed by you or your customer. Using various natural remedies is a great alternative, but many will not exclude insects that can be beneficial to your crops. Most pest determinants for keeping bugs away will keep all bugs away, the good and the bad.

Tackle Weeds Early

Weeds are not only unsightly; they will steal away vital nutrients and water from the soil that your crops need to grow. Weeds can quickly become a problem and, if left unattended, will smooth out your crops, leaving you with a field of unproductive plants. Tilling your fields can help reduce weed growth before you begin planting and as your crops are growing.

Rotating crops and planting in different areas of your farm can help minimize pest and weed problems, and this can be beneficial to the soil as well. Knowing how to start your crops right under the best conditions and then nurturing them until harvest is vital for your farm's success. To maintain your farm for years to come, however, there are other elements you need to take care of. In the next chapter, you will learn that caring for your crops begins with caring for your land.

Chapter 6:
Caring For Your Land

You will need to ensure you have suitable land to plant in for years to come, and this requires a great deal of focus on ensuring the soil is well nourished. The hard work does not start with the plant but in the prepping prior to planting. You will have to create the right growing environment and implement the proper growing techniques to grow a successful and abundant harvest. This chapter will walk you through the various options for getting the soil ready to nourish the seeds or plants you place in the ground.

Fertilizing Your Soil

A bountiful crop begins with healthy soil. Before you plant your first crop, you need to test the fertility levels. Having proper fertility levels before you plant is vital because once you plant, it is incredibly difficult to make adjustments to achieve better levels. Testing should be done in the early spring and late fall. Fertility levels can vary from one area of the field to another, so you should test a few areas to get a better understanding of what the soil needs to maintain higher levels of fertility. After the first initial testing, you will want to check fertility levels every three years.

During the colder months is when you want to apply a healthy layer of fertilizer to your soil. Fertilizer feeds the soil, and the soil will feed your plants. Well fertilized soil will ensure maximum crop production. This process will take trial and error and can change from year to year. How much fertilizer you, the type of fertilizer you use, and when you apply will have an impact on the soil fertility.

There are few things that can impact soil fertility levels. These include:

- Soil ecosystem

- Minerals- soil contains three core minerals; clay, sand, and silt

- Microbials

Fertilized soil will have the right balance of nitrogen, phosphorus, potassium, magnesium, and calcium. When choosing a fertilizer, you'll want to ensure it contains the appropriate levels of these nutrients. If soil contains too much or too little of these nutrients, it can be difficult to grow healthy crops. Compost is also a type of fertilizer that you can apply after you have planted your crops and while they are growing.

Organizing Your Land

You don't want to just plant in an open field. Constructing the right setup for where you will grow will keep your crops organized and easy to find. Always start with a plan. For organizing your crops and tracking the success of your growing season, a diagram can be helpful. Draw out the lay of your land and map out where you will put each crop when they will be or have been planted, and how long before you can anticipate harvesting to start.

Tilling Practices

A till is used to prepare the land for planting and can be used to turn the soil to mix old soil with fertilizer or mulch, which will add and distribute nutrients back into the soil. This process helps break up the soil, prevent weed growth, and keep pests away from crops. Tilling should not be done if conditions are too wet. This will only cause the soil to smear and will not create an adequate bed for laying seeds or planting starter plants. There are three popular tilling practices you should be aware of.

1. Conventional tillage

Conventional tillage involves multiple passes of a till through the crop field, before, during, and after the growing season. This approach to till regularly disturbs the soil and can allow for seedlings to emerge sooner than with other tilling methods. This can get your crops growing faster. Conventional tilling also uses a till to keep weeds out of hand away from growing plants until they reach a certain height.

1. Minimal tillage

This tilling practice can allow you to sow your crops sooner than conventional tillage, and crops also tend to have higher yields. This practice cuts back on tilling unless necessary or when preparing the land for sowing. Minimal tilling lowers the disruption to the soil, which can help it improve over time.

1. Zero or no-tillage

No-till farming does not use tillage to grow crops from year to year. While no-till crops do have a greater risk of being overrun with weeds, this can be more beneficial to the soil. Not tilling the land means you can sow your crops much sooner. No-till farming will also allow you to plant fall crops much sooner as you won't have to put off sowing seeds due to the soil being too wet and not doing what it is supposed to do. If using this method, there are additional measures you need to take to ensure the soil remains healthy each growing season, though this is not much different than what you should already be doing. The most important process to include with a no-till approach is crop rotation, which will be discussed a little later in this book.

Tilling can instantly improve the quality of the soil you plant in, but tilling should only be done when it is needed. Over time, excessive tiling will cause the quality of your soil to decline. This is because nutrients will be lost, and the structure of the soil will change, causing an increase in erosion.

When deciding which tilling approach to take, you should take into consideration the following:

- Soil composition
- Weeds
- Organic matter
- Water management
- Soil biology
- Crop rotation

To keep a farm successful, it is wise to adopt some no-till practice to maintain healthy land for years to come.

Proper Sun Exposure

All crops will need sun exposure for proper growth. The plant's ability to absorb sunlight will depend on the surface area of the plant's leaves. Leaf disease, insects, and weeds can interfere with leaf surface area and reduce the amount of sun that the plant will absorb. Therefore, the more light it can obtain, the better the crops will grow.

Planting seeds at the right time can ensure crops get sufficient sunlight to produce a high yield for harvest time. Seeds planted earlier when days are getting longer and have more sun exposure will give crops an advantage over crops planted later in the season when longer daylight hours will only last for a few weeks before becoming shorter.

Sun exposure will impact plant temperatures. While most farmers are always concerned and pay close attention to low temperatures and frost, high temperatures will also negatively affect crop growth. If the temperature rises too much, photosynthesis can halt, resulting in low to no yield for harvesting. Therefore, during periods of high temperature, you will need to take extra precautionary steps to keep your plant temperatures at a lower temperature which can include setting up a temporary shade or misting water systems to fields.

Water Concerns

Moisture plays a crucial role in seed germination. Most seeds will need 30 percent of their weight in water. Too much water and the seed will rot, while too little water and the seed will split and dry out. You will also need to ensure there is proper drainage on the land, so excess water flows away from the roots. If plant roots sit in flooded soil, the roots will begin to rot, and when the roots rot, the rest of the crop will rot too. Minerals found in the soil play a crucial role in proper water drainage. Soil that has an equal sand and clay ratio will make it easier for excess water to drain away from the crops. If the soil has too much clay, the water will sit. If the soil has too much sand, water will escape too quickly, and the roots won't have a chance to get enough water when it is needed.

Plants use water to help with the photosynthesis process but also rely on it to help keep leaf surfaces cool. Water is released through the stomata of the leaf, which reduces the heat stress placed on the leaf.

During the germination stage of plant life, it will require more water than it may have survived during the beginning, pre-germination stage. Each plant will require different amounts of water to thrive, and you will need to factor in other elements that can hinder water absorption by the roots. Once a plant has reached maturity, water absorption declines significantly.

Two main water concerns every farmer should be prepared to face are drought and flooding. Drought is when there is a serious lack of water available to the crops. Droughts can occur when temperatures remain above the expected average temperature for days, weeks, or months at a time. If there are lower precipitation levels, then a drought may occur. Severe and mild drought conditions can reduce your crop yield by 50 percent or more.

Flooding can take out your current and future crops if you do not address any issue prior to planting. While there is no way to avoid flooding when substantial amounts of rain begin to fall, or rain keeps falling down for days, there are a few things you can do to better prepare yourself and your farm for the hard hit.

First, review your farmers' insurance and check if flood damage or loss is covered. If not, ask to have it added. If the company is unable to add this to your policy, try to find another company that can.

Next, address your drainage systems. If you do not have a drainage system in place, it is time to consider one seriously. If a system is already in place, make routine checks of the system to ensure there is nothing obstructing water flow. It is common for debris and sediments to accumulate in channels and screens, which impair the system's effectiveness.

Finally, consider adding or improving water drainage systems on your farm with some of the suggestions below.

- Low-grade weirs or other water control structures

- In-ditch conservation systems

- Downstream systems

- Pipes that are designed with in-field slot

- Riser with boards to control water movement

- Upgrade or improve water infiltration systems

- Add year-round plants to slow water flow around crops

- Protect crops using sandbags or putting up temporary barriers when you know long periods of rain are about to occur

Soil Health and Nutrition

Soil is more than just the dirt you will plant in. Soil contains minerals, water, organic matter, air, and live organisms, all of which can impact your corps. You will want to ensure that the soil is the pH for the plants you grow. pH levels are a measure of how alkaline or acidic the soil is, and this will influence the nutrients and microbes present in the soil. Most crops grow well in slightly alkaline soil because this type of environment preserves the nutrients available for plant absorption. There are plenty of ways you can supply the soil with nutrients and steps you can take to ensure healthy soil.

Making Your Own Compost

Making your own compost is cost-efficient and often a more effective way to supply your crops with proper nutrients. For organic farmers, homemade compost lets you have complete control over what is going into the soil to feed your plants.

When making compost, use the dried leaves, grass clipping, and lawn debris gathered from your farm or lawn. The compost you make yourself will have a rougher quality to it than store-bought compost. This is a good sign that the compost contains living microbes that are essential for plant life and growth. A lot of the compost you buy from a supplier will have a decent amount of nutrients, but most will lack the vital microbial. Homemade compost also allows you to customize compost to include more of the nutrients the soil in your field needs, leading to higher-yielding crops. If you test your soil and notice the pH levels are too low, you can add in an alkaline matter to bring the levels up.

Homemade compost often does a much better job of slowing down or stopping soil erosion. It also adds waterways within the soil, and this prevents the topsoil of the ground from baking and cracking when exposed to too much sunlight.

Creating your own compost can also be better for the environment and help with climate control. Store-bought compost is made using large, heavy machines that use up a lot of fuel and release a lot of carbon into the atmosphere. When you make compost yourself, you are cutting back on how much fuel and energy waste goes into manufacturer compost.

Homemade Compost Steps

There are two types of compost you can make for your farm.

1. Cold compost uses various uncooked food scraps and organic material. These materials are placed into a large bin with a little bit of ground soil and then stored for a year. In the year time frame, the matter begins to decompose, and when it is done, you have rich compost to use on your farm.

2. Hot compost is similar to cold compost, but the process takes just a few months as opposed to a year. With warm composting, you need four main ingredients to create your material: carbon, air, water, and nitrogen. You can also create a

vermicompost with this method by adding redworms or red wigglers to the compost.

You can choose to use one or both of these methods to have plenty of compost to use on your farm year-round. With hot composting, you will want to make two batches a year, one to use at the beginning of your growing season and one to make at the end.

Scrapes and matter you can use in your compost include:

- Uncooked food scraps such as fruit and vegetable peels

- Coffee grinds

- Eggshells (these should be dried and then crushed before adding to your compost bin as they can take much longer to break down than other matter)

- Grass clipping

- Dry leaves

- Plant clippings

- Finely chopped wood and bark chips

- Straw

- Untreated wood sawdust

Things to avoid using in your compost bins:

- Cooked foods

- Raw meats or poultry

- Citrus fruit peels or scraps (this can repel earthworms)

- Onion or garlic scraps (can repel earthworms)

- Foods scraps that have oil or grease on them

- Plant clippings from diseases plants

- Pressure-treated wood sawdust or chips

- Weeds that will produce seeds after they have died

- Dairy products

- Domestic animal feces (dog or cat feces)

Now that you know what you should and should not include in your composting, follow the steps below to make your own homemade compost.

For hot compost:

1. Have a large enough bin or bins to properly keep your compost. Compost bins can be essay constructed out of pallets, or you can buy large containers and bins for composting.

2. You will start with gathering enough brown material first. For hot compost that will be ready in three to six months, have at least a three-foot pile of brown material. This material will be dried grass and leaves, tree branches, bark, and other dried natural materials. This is the carbon component of your hot compost.

3. Lay green materials on top of the brown. Green materials refer to your kitchen scraps, fresh cut grass clippings, and plant trimmings. The green materials add nitrogen to your compost. When combining the brown and green material, keep it at

a three to one ratio, three parts brown, one part green. You are just layering the materials at this point. You can do a few layers of each just to be sure to maintain the proper ratio of brown to green matter.

4. If the compost looks as though it contains too much moisture or is wet, add in more brown materials. If the mixture is too brown or very dry, add more green materials.

5. Water your compost regularly. Your composition should feel damp and warm but not wet. Adding too much water to your compost will cause it to rot and not decay properly.

6. You should keep track of the temperature of your compost to ensure it is not becoming too warm or wet and cold using a simple garden thermometer. Your compost should remain close to 130 degrees and not go above 150 degrees Fahrenheit.

7. When your compost does reach a temperature between 130 and 150 degrees Fahrenheit, you will need to stir it. Stirring helps minimize the odor that can occur when composting, but it also speeds up the composting process. You will continue to stir the compost at least once a week or as needed when it reaches the right temperature.

8. Your hot compost will be ready when you have a dark brown mixture that is dry and crumbling. When compost has fully cooked, the temperature should not rise, and the mixture should not be giving off heat.

For cold compost:

1. Start by setting up your compost bins or a storage area. Try to place your compost bins in a shaded area.

2. You will add material to your bins as they become available.

3. Start with dry leaves and clippings. If you have a large pile of dried leaves, do not add them all at once. Save some to layer on top of other scraps you add through the weeks. When adding kitchen scraps later, keep them towards the center of the compost bin. You do not have to worry about maintaining a certain ratio of materials.

4. As with hot compost, keep the mixture damp by adding water or fresh grass clippings. If an odor begins to waft from the bin, use a garden fork to flip the materials and allow more oxygen in.

Outdoor temperatures will have an impact on how quickly or slowly it takes for your compost to become ready. Those farming in warmer clients where the temperature stays above freezing will find their compost is ready in a short time. Farmers in colder climates, where the temperature drops below freezing overnight or in the day, will find it can take months longer for compost to be ready. Cold composting is better for those in colder climates who do not need to have compost ready or on hand for planting since there may be months where you are unable to plant.

At the beginning of your planting season, apply about six inches of compost to your fields. You can add more throughout the growing season if your soil is lacking proper nutrients.

Any leftover compost you have can be used to make a compost tea. To do this, you will use unfinished compost. Place the compost into a cloth bag. You do not want the material to escape, but you do want water to beagle to flow through the bag and the material. Place these bags of compost into a bin and fill it with water. Leave the compost to steep in the water for three days. When steeping is finished, you can use the water as a liquid fertilizer on your plants.

Crop Rotations

Crop rotation is the practice of planting different crops in the same area right after each other. This is done to allow the new crop to take advantage of the residue and nutrients left behind from the previous crop. In addition, crop rotations can restore certain elements from the soil to maintain a healthy balance. For example, if you plant a crop that absorbs a significant amount of nitrogen from the soil, you will want to plant a crop after it supplies the soil with nitrogen. Many farmers use this method to help improve soil health instead of using fertilizers. This can cut back on business expenses since you do not have to spend on fertilizers as often or as much as you typically would.

Since crops will also have different root systems, planting crops with a deep roots system followed by a crop with a shallow roots system will prevent the soil from becoming depleted. This approach also helps improve drainage and water retention of the soil.

Farmers can benefit from a crop rotation plan because it allows them to consistently have something growing and ready to harvest all year round. Diversifying crops in this manner can protect you from economic hardships and a steady stream of income. This also allows you to make money and improve the physical components of the land. You may also find that consistent crop rotation produces higher-yielding crops.

Cover Crops

Cover crops are plants you grow to improve the health of the soil. These crops help fertilize the soil, add organic matter, attract beneficial insects to the field, and change the nutrient value of the land. Cover crops can be planted at any time and will protect the soil from remaining bare, which will cause nutrient loss. They also help prevent weed growth and topsoil erosion. You can use these crops for long-term benefits or short-term boosts to soil health.

Long-term cover crops like oats, barley, and legumes are some of the best plants to use. Short-term cover crops should be quick-growing crops that will overpower weed growth. Buckwheat and field peas are two of the most commonly used short-term cover crops favored by farmers. The right cover crop you use will depend on a few factors such as:

- When do you next plan to plant? If you want to plant seeds right away, short-term cover crops like buckwheat are recommended.

- What types of crops will you plant? Different cover crops will release chemicals as they decompose, and this can cause certain crops to be unsuccessful when planted after the cover crop.

- Are you planting in the summer or winter? Different cover crops will be more effective depending on the season they are planted in. Clovers and Austrian pea are better for winter. Soybeans and cowpeas are better suited for summer.

When planting cover crops, you will want the plants to become as mature as possible but not mature enough where they produce seeds. Once the plant has slightly surpassed optimal maturity, kill it by mowing it or chopping it down. The crop then becomes a mulch for the land, providing it with ample food and nutrients as it decomposes.

When you are planting seeds, the temperature of the soil will have an impact on where the seed will germinate or become dormant.

Buffer Zones

Buffer zones are dedicated areas of land that have permanent vegetation or flowing water. This vegetation maintains the air, water, and soil quality of the surrounding land. Buffer zones are also essential for organic farming. They provide a protective barrier for your crops against contamination or substance from infiltrating your crops.

There are no guidelines stating how big buffer zones need to be, just that they are doing their job of keeping contamination out of organic farming zones. These areas can contain any number of vegetation and are best with a diverse combination of plant life. You can grow crops for harvesting in buffer zones, though these crops will not be eligible for organic certification. The slope of the land will have an impact on buffer zone effectiveness, and this is important to consider when choosing plants to keep here.

Even if you will not intend to farm organically grown produce, it is a good idea to have buffer zones or stripes on your land. These areas provide a natural habitat for wildlife, and this can keep them away from your growing crops. Buffers can also help you maintain healthy soil throughout your land because they help control soil erosion due to wind or water. They also improve soil quality. Consider buffer zones like the shingles on your home. They provide protection and curb appeal. Once in place, they take little maintenance unless you are harvesting in the area.

Growing and Staying Organic

If you plan on producing crops that will be labeled as organic, there are guidelines you need to follow. These guidelines are applied to the land you intend to use for your crops, soil quality, water availability, and other processes for growing and harvesting organic crops.

Requirements for Organic Farms

While this is not an exhaustive list, the following requirements will help you prepare your land now for organic growing. As you implement the following requirement, you should take this time to become further educated on organic farming and best practices.

Land Requirements

There are two major land requirements when growing organic crops.

1. The land you plan on using must be free from prohibited substances for three years. If a substance was used on your land last year and you want to grow organic tomatoes this year, you won't be able to. You will need to wait another two years before the crop would be considered organic.

2. The land needs to have buffer zones around the perimeter of the crops to protect and prevent unintentional contamination from prohibited substances. This is especially important if you have land next to other farmers that are not organic certified.

Soil Fertility and Nutrient Requirements

Organic farmers need to take extra care of their soil and be careful how they implement traditional farming methods. Here are some things to be aware of when it comes to soil fertility and nutrient management.

- Tilling and cultivation practice must improve or at the very least maintain soil condition.

- Practice must minimize soil erosion.

- Soil management techniques cannot use chemical methods. Crop rotations, cover crops, and organic plant or animal fertilizer should be used instead.

- Farmers must be careful that crop, soil, and water contamination does not occur when using raw manure to improve soil health.

- Sewage sludge is prohibited.

- Compost must adhere to the National Organic Program (NOP) composting process guidelines.

Seeds and Plant Requirements

There are various rules and guidelines that deal with seeds and the types of plants that can be grown on an organic farm. While it is recommended that you familiarize yourself with the regulations, a standard rule to follow is that seeds and plants that will produce edible crops must be organic.

Organic Crop Rotation Requirements

Your farm must have a crop rotation plan that includes cover crops, green manure crops, catch crops, and sod crops. Crop rotation must be performed to improve the organic matter in the soil, replenish or balance plant nutrients, reduce soil erosion, and control the pest.

Pest and Disease Management Requirements

Integrated pest management (IPM) systems are required on organic farms. These systems are in place for pest control, weed control, and disease prevention. Practices that adhere to IPM requirements include:

- Crop rotations.

- Incorporating plant varieties on land that have a built-in resistance to pests, weeds, and disease.

- Developing a natural habitat to introduce parasites or other predators that are enemies of the pests.

- Using non-synthetic methods such as traps or lures.

- Using biodegradable mulch.

- Livestock grazing for weed control.

Being Certified

To become a certified organic farm, there are a few steps you need to take to obtain the certification.

1. You must have an organic system plan. This plan outlines how your farm will operate under certified organic systems. All practices used for soil health, preparing the land, crop selection, and growing methods are key components of your plan that need to be detailed and well-organized.

2. Cet your plan review by a certified agent and begin implementing it. These agents can be found all over the world.

3. Have your farming operation inspected by a certifying agent. This will be a thorough, in-depth inspection that will review every component of your farming business and everything located on the land. The inspection will look at the field you are growing in to ensure it meets certified organic measures. It will test soil conditions and crop health. Inspecting agents will review weed, pest,

and soil health management systems as well as water systems, equipment, and storage areas. Be prepared for this to be a long process.

4. Once the inspection is complete, you will want to review it with a certifying agent. The agent who did the inspection will have created thorough reports and analyses that pertain to the risk of contamination, preventative measures, and assessment of all systems in place. Another agent will review all this data and guide you to things that need to be improved, addressed, or are not in compliance with organic requirements.

5. If your farm is found to comply with all regulations, you will be issued an organic certification. Once certified, you will need to continue to update your organic system plan as you make modifications to your farm. Every year, you will be subject to another inspection to ensure that your farm is still adhering to organic regulations. These follow-up inspections are necessary to maintain your organic certification status.

Time Investment

Managing a farm will take a full-time commitment. Tending and caring for your crops is a time-consuming process, but there are other things you will need to spend your time on as well. For example, obtaining an organic certification will require additional effort and attention to detail. To make a profit with your farm, you will need to understand, be prepared, and be willing to put the time into daily operations.

Patience will be your greatest skill as you continue with your farming business. Knowing how to handle problems and resolve them in a timely manner will be another core skill that can lead to the success or demise of your farm. You will need to be able to properly assess when problems need to be fixed right away so you can continue with your work or step out for a day or two while you focus on something else.

Chapter 7:
Prepping Your Crop for The Market

Now that you have a clear idea of what crops you will grow, the system you will use, and have planned out your goals, you need to take a vision to your market. As mentioned earlier, growing and harvesting are only part of the farming equation. Getting your produce from the farm to the people is the other half. This requires a clear sense of your market and marketing plan and a fail-proof system for ensuring that your customer gets what they order from you. In this final chapter, we will take a look at the other essentials for building and maintaining a successful business.

Is The Market Ready for You?

This is a crucial component of the whole process. You ideally want to ensure key factors are already in place before you begin harvesting, but if you have neglected any of the components in this section, you need to address them now.

Do You Have Customers?

We discussed understanding your market when drafting your business plan, but just because there is a market does not mean you immediately have a customer base to rely on. There can be a demand for what you grow, but if no one knows that you meet their demands, you will be left with an abundance of crops and nowhere to move them.

It's crucial to build awareness around your business to attract the right customers. When you imagine the people who will buy your produce, who are they? Men, women, younger people, retired individuals? You want to know specific details about your market that will help you craft an effective marketing plan to attract these people. If you are growing various products, you might have a different audience for each product. This is important to note as you will want to have a plan in place to reach each of these markets.

Build an Online Presence

If you want your farming business to take off, then it needs to have an online presence. You will need a website first to direct people to so they can learn more about your farm. If you plan on having online ordering options, you need to ensure your website is set up for eCommerce.

You also need to embrace social media. Social media is one of the easiest and fast ways you can begin to build an online presence. The potential for you to reach thousands of people is remarkable, but you need to understand the best practices for each platform. You do not need to set up an account on every platform that is available, but it doesn't hurt to create a solid presence of two or three. If you lack social media marketing skills, you can always hire someone with more knowledge and understanding to boost your presence. If it is not in your budget to hire someone, there are three general rules to follow:

1. Be consistent. You need to post every day to get more views on your profile, and some platforms favor accounts that post multiple times a day.

2. Share before you sell. A majority of what you post on your social media accounts will be about adding value to your audience, not promoting your products. As a general rule, no more than ten percent of your post should promote your business.

3. Focus on engagement. Asked questions in your post, get people to share your post with others, and always respond to comments that are left. The more engagement your post gets, the more views your profile will get.

It is best to create a social media schedule to help you stay on track with your marketing goals. Sit down once a week to map out what you will post and then create a draft of as many of these posts, so they are ready to share when you have scheduled them. Leave room in your schedule to add some live videos or images, so your profile looks and feels more authentic.

Also, consider blogging or vlogging. These avenues can provide people with more information about what you do and why. They will allow you to connect with your market on a deeper level and not just one where you are trying to sell to them. Blogs and vlogs are a great way to share your message and educate people on sustainable living. What you post through your blog or vlog will also give you more content to share on your social media accounts.

Proper Cleaning

You need to have the proper wash system in place when you are selling your harvest. There should be wash stations located on your land so you can quickly go from harvesting to deliveries. You will want a dunk wash for leafy vegetables, which consists of tanks of water for soaking certain vegetables and gently dunking others. A spray wash system is essential for root vegetables to remove dirt. You also need a drying table to set your vegetables after washing so you are not packing them wet, which will cause bacteria and mold growth.

Using vinegar in your produce cleaning wash will remove any residue that has found its way onto the produce, either intentionally or unintentionally. It does an excellent job of breaking up wax that can build up on the outer layers of the produce. Vinegar also prevents bacterial growth, ensuring that the produce stays fresh longer.

There are plenty of ways to set up a washing station. You just need to decide what is the most efficient and effective one for you. Many farmers set up converter belts to wash root vegetables. Others have multiple soaking tanks to clean more of their harvest all at once. You may find that these methods do not thoroughly clean the produce as they should or combine methods to save time. It does not matter which options you choose, but you do need to clean your produce before storing them or packaging them for deliveries.

How To Sell?

Know the options you have to sell your produce. At first, you may stick with selling your crops as whole fresh fruits and vegetables. You might set up a stand at the farmers' market because this is the only available option you have. There are several ways you can sell what you grow aside from farmers' markets. There are also additional ways you can expand on what you sell. While you will need to do additional research and educate yourself further on the legal requirements, it is wise to recognize that there are plenty of opportunities to establish a successful farm in more than one way.

Selling Locally

Many beginners begin to gain a loyal customer base by selling to friends, family, neighbors, and anyone else they know in the immediate community. This is a great place to get started, but it does come with a list of drawbacks and frustration. Family and friends may be eager to support you but, as human nature often is, they may expect a substantial discount or not feel pressure to pay in full when you deliver their goods. This can cause some tension within your relationships. While it is not discouraged to start this way, make sure you make it clear that you are operating a business and that your loved ones and those closest to you should treat your transaction as they would with any other business.

Community-Supported Agriculture (CSA)

CSAs are subscription services that customers sign up for either as a monthly or seasonal agreement. The customer pays upfront for a percentage of the farm's harvest for the season. These subscriptions allow you to establish a great connection with your customer. The customer already pays for the crop before you even plant for the season, and these can eliminate your need to borrow money. There are a few ways you can set up successful CSAs. First, you want to start with a small customer poll. The size of your land will depend on how big this poll is. Most startup farms will do well with about 30 customers. Each customer will pay their subscription and, for the dedicated time (typically the length of the season, six or seven months), will receive their percentage of produce delivered on a weekly basis. Deliveries on average equate to around ten pounds of produce for each person.

A slightly different approach is instead of delivering the produce, the customer will come to your farm and pick up their deliveries. You can allow for items to be swapped out or traded, so customers leave with exactly what they want.

You can ensure that you grow the produce customers want by sending out a list of crops you are considering and gain feedback from these subscribers for what they would want.

CSAs are a great way to retain customers, but the biggest drawback of these is finding customers who will pay for the subscription before receiving the product.

Selling Wholesale

There are many wholesale opportunities for farmers. Grocery stores, health-food stores, and other chain stores can provide you an additional outlet to sell your produce. It is not always easy to get your product or products into the wholesale arena. It can also be more stressful to guarantee and then follow through on supplying these stores with the quantity of product they expect. If you are considering going in the wholesale direction, consider consignment sales. These will often carry a higher profit.

Local Restaurants

Restaurants are always in need of produce, and they can provide a great opportunity for farmers. Your best bet for landing an agreement with a restaurant is to seek out specialty locations that have staff chefs. These types of local restaurants tend to care more about using fresh whole foods in their dishes. You might struggle to find a restaurant that does not already work with a local farmer if there are plenty of farms in your area, but there will be occasions when the other farm might not come through with a delivery, and you can be the one they call. Get your name and business out and into the mix. You will also have a better chance of establishing a relationship with restaurants if you have specialty crops which can be a great selling point.

When looking for restaurants, do not be afraid to approach those in more touristy areas. These locations will have more people dining at their establishment, and the restaurants will need to make bigger orders to serve their customers, which results in better profit for you. If you do not get an immediate yes from the restaurants, you can still gain new customers by sharing with the owners and other employees other ways they can buy from you.

If you do arrange a deal with a restaurant, also ensure the produce you supply them is clean and looks good. The most important thing to keep in mind is that you have to supply what the restaurant has ordered. If you do not follow through in being able to fulfill their request for a certain quantity, they will drop you as a supplier quickly. Not receiving the full delivery can result in dishes unable to be made or only being able to make a limited number of dishes that might be one of their best selling. This costs the restaurant money. If you can not supply what you promised to deliver, then do not make the promise to do so.

Trade Shows and Fairs

Trade shows and fairs are similar to a farmers' market but are a greater opportunity to promote your farm and what you supply to a larger audience. You can set up a booth to attract people to your booth, where you will have brochures, flyers, and additional ways for people to take with them how to contact you. You might even offer more than just samples of your produce or products like a cooking lesson to showcase how to create healthy and satisfying meals with your produce and products.

Chances are there are plenty of trade shows and fairs taking place in your area, and you can find out when they are happening and how to become a part of it by contacting your local chamber of commerce. Do not limit yourself to obvious farm or craft shows. Consider festivals, food fairs, and other opportunities that can get your business more attention.

To participate in most shows and fairs, you will need to pay a booth fee. These can vary from 25 dollars to over 200 dollars, and if you have to travel far to attend the show, you will have to take into consideration money spent on gas and possibly staying at a hotel since these can run late into the day. You might not make back what you put into attending these shows, so choose them carefully. If there is a greater potential for you to bring in a small profit off of items you sell, you might want to consider setting up a booth once a month or every other month.

Catalog Sales

After a few years running your farming business successfully, you may have begun to branch out and started offering additional products aside from what you grow. If you have a variety of value-added products such as sauces, jams, candies, or salsa, you can create a catalog to send out or display on your website for people to order from. This venture will require more time, investment, and patience. You will need to juggle the influx of orders from the catalog, shipping the items, and often making the items on demand, and you will still need to accomplish all your normal tasks for maintaining your farm. While this option lets you use the produce you grow in different ways, and lets you use other selling options, you need to ensure you will be ready for the commitment and additional stress that can come along with selling value-adding products in this way.

Delivering Products

While you have been busy making connections, getting businesses and the locals interested in your farming products, have you considered how you will get the product from your farm to distributors? What types of delivery services will you offer? There are plenty of opportunities to attract more customers with delivery services your farm offers, but you need to understand the commitment and obstacles that may arise by trying to do too much. A home delivery service can provide customers an easy and more convenient way to purchase your products.

Establishing a Delivery Service

For home delivery options, you need to establish criteria for order placements. Before setting up guidelines for home deliveries, get feedback from your market. Ask what kind of services they would be interested in a fresh produce delivery and what things they would absolutely not be ok with. Getting feedback from your target audience will help you cater your services to what they want, which can lead to much greater success.

To help you set up a home delivery service, consider the following suggestions:

- Your website will serve as a central hub for customers to request deliveries. You need to keep your website up to date, so it provides your customer with a list of items you have or will have available for delivery.

- Be sure your website is mobile-friendly. People spend most of their time on their phones, not in front of their computers. It is important that your website is incredibly user-friendly for mobile devices.

- Create bundle delivery options. Some people love a lot of choices, but most consumers want a few options to choose from so they can order and be done.

- Consider subscription services for your deliveries. Have offers for weekly deliveries of produce that customers use often and won't keep for longer than a few days.

- Ensure your payment method requires deliveries to be paid in full at the time the order is placed. Consider adding a delivery fee to orders as well. You'll want to charge a little extra so you can cover gas and set some of the delivery revenue into a repair savings account that can be used to take care of work you may need to get done on your delivery vehicle.

- Keep your home delivery services restricted to just a small area.

- When just starting your delivery service, have set days that deliveries will take place on, like, Monday, Wednesday, and Saturday. Try to keep delivery to a time period, 12 noon to 6 pm. Once you have a comfortable handle on local deliveries, you can begin to add on more delivery locations.

Keep in mind, if you are in the process of gaining organic certifications, how you store and transport your produce will need to meet organic guidelines.

For delivery services, you will need to consider investing in delivery vans that are climate-controlled. You can make small local deliveries with your farm truck if you have proper storage and transportation systems in place. For large deliveries or when shipping to a location that is slightly further away, you will need to have the proper van to keep the produce cool, so they arrive fresh. If buying a van upfront is not an option, look into renting a delivery van instead. Know how many are available, the cost, and when you need to put in a request to ensure you have it on hand when you need it.

Growing Your Business

Growing your farming business can take on many forms. You can grow by focusing on gaining more customers, you can grow by offering more services or products, or you can grow by becoming more efficient in the daily tasks to run the farm.

Reinvesting Your Profits

1. Once you have a handle on cultivating an easy and standard crop, consider reinvesting some of your profits to include more specialized crops.

2. Use profits to purchase equipment or machines that can speed up some of the farming processes.

3. Consider how else your land can be used. If you have a barn on the land, turning it into a bed and breakfast location can bring you in some extra money.

4. If you have spare land, consider using it for livestock or create a luxurious space to breed dogs, goats, rabbits, or other animals.

5. If you grow grapes, consider learning how to make wine to sell. This opens up a few other ways to get

more out of your farm. You can offer tasting, wine classes, and tours of the vineyard. The same is true if you grow hops which you can use to make craft beers. You will need to reinvest a bit to obtain the proper machinery. If you don't have grape crops, this might be a great place to put extra funds into.

6. Reinvest profits into starting a nursery. If you have the extra land to dedicate to growing flower varieties, a nursery offers many new streams of income.

Expand Your Reach

Listen to what your customers want, and then do what you can to provide it to them. Think outside the box when you visualize your ideal customer. Your target audience does not have to be limited to just one group. Take into consideration individuals who would be investing in seeing your farm grow. For example, college athletes in your area may have a greater interest in your organic product than the rest of the student body. Individuals struggling with health problems can become loyal customers if you provide them an easy way to take control of their health by choosing better foods for them. Moms of picky eaters may love your marketing ideas that speak to their picky eating kids to encourage them to eat their veggies.

Do not be afraid to embrace technology in other areas of yore farming procedures. There are apps and gadgets that will help you find imperfections in your land, give you instant solutions for crop issues, and create a better system to maximize your harvest yield. Investing some of your profits into new technology can be a smart way to see significant returns on your investment.

Creating Effective Systems

Having the right operating systems in place will make running your business much easier. These systems should allow you or anyone else to complete your dairy farming tanks and other recurring obligations without hesitation. These systems are also in place to provide a backup plan when things are not going as expected, such as when weather interrupts your workday or cuts your crop in half. Operations plans will help stop a crisis from becoming out of control.

Continually educate yourself and experiment with different growing and harvesting techniques that can help you streamline your corp availability. If something works great, find ways to make it work better. If something did not work at all, find a way to make it work better. You will not always have the luxury of trying one thing, and if it does not work, move on to something different. When you are just starting your farm, you need to work with what you have, and that means making those things work in the most efficient manner.

Branding Yourself

Creating a brand is the best way to ensure a loyal and long-term customer base. If you focus on having positive interactions with customers, distributors, and other merchants, more people will want to do business with you.

You will want to set your farm apart from another located in your community. To do this, you will have to look at your operations and highlight what your farm is doing differently. Establish a unique sell proposition that you can use to showcase why customers will benefit from choosing your products over others. This can reflect your mission statement.

Building a brand is about building the right reputation. What you build that reputation around depends on you. You can establish a reputation of always being friendly yet professional. Your reputation might reflect your nature and how you are always looking for ways to give back or educate the community. Your reputation may be focused on a topic that you are passionate about.

Let your passion and why guide your brand identity and reputation. People will be naturally drawn to you and your business because of your dedication and enthusiasm. If you show up consistently with that passion and drive, the market will follow. Consistency is key. Once you have established your farming business and yourself as an expert or leader of change around one topic, you need to consistently support your message.

It is important that as you are building your brand that you remain authentic in your interactions. If educating others about sustainable living and showing them how they can become more self-sufficient in their own land is not something that lights a fire in your heart, do not try to push the cause on yourself or others. Also, remember there is more to your farm and you than your mission. Let your customer and anyone else you do business with getting to know you.

Conclusion

Farming is hard work but fulfilling work. If you can picture your life five or ten years from now, would you rather be sitting behind a desk in some office building or sitting behind the wheel of your tractor looking over endless fields of nourishing foods? If the first is more appealing to you than enjoying your comfy office chair. If the latter is what you envision, it is time to turn it into a reality.

Owning your own small-scale farm is not a side hustle. It is a full business undertaking. You need to be confident and comfortable with the time commitments required of you if you want to make a substantial profit. Be willing to embrace your farming endeavor as a learning process and be a lifetime learner. Stay up to date about the farming technologies, methods, and advancements that will lead to more profitability and less effort. This consistent effort to learn will move you from a beginner farmer to a successful farmer.

This book has provided you with an in-depth look at what it takes to start your own farming business. You have learned the tools and equipment needed to make operating your farm more efficient. You know what documents to obtain to run your business legally. You have all the information you need to go from a blank canvas of land to a self-sustaining business. Now, it is time to put this information to use.

Create a plan. Create a vision. Get up every day with passion fueling your day, and you will find the hard work rewarding in more ways than you can imagine.

We hope this book has provided you with clarity and excitement around the possibilities that can arise from starting your own small farm. We hope that you share what you have learned with others and put to use the information on these pages. If you have found value in what you learn here, we encourage you to leave a review and let others know how you have learned and grown as a farmer. We thank you and wish you luck and success on your new, exciting journey!

References

5 easy steps to make door-to-door delivery profitable for your farm. (2020, April 4). BARN2DOOR. https://www.barn2door.com/blog/5-easy-steps-to-make-door-to-door-delivery-profitable-for-your-farm

7 essential crop care tips for first-time farmers. (2018, November 27). BARNDOOR. https://barndoorag.com/barn-blog/7-essential-crop-care-tips-for-firsttime-farmers/

7 reasons why small farms fail. (n.d.). Small Farm Nation. https://smallfarmnation.com/7-reason-why-small-farms-fail/

Agridirect.ie. (2018, January 3). *Why being a farmer is the best occupation in the world.* Agri Direct. https://www.agridirect.ie/blog/why-being-a-farmer-is-the-best-occupation-in-the-world/

Anderson, S. (2016, August 26). *3 tips to successfully hire farm workers.* Farm Progress. https://www.farmprogress.com/blogs-3-tips-successfully-hire-farm-workers-11272

Arcuri, L. (2020, November 21). *Writing your own small farm business plan.* Treehugger. https://www.treehugger.com/write-a-small-farm-business-plan-3016944

B & G Garden Editors. (2020, September 9). *We've broken down the science of composting for you.* Better Homes & Gardens.

https://www.bhg.com/gardening/yard/compost/how-to-compost/

Baker, B. (2018, March 29). *How you can reduce flood risk on your farm.* Farm Progress. https://www.farmprogress.com/land-management/how-you-can-reduce-flood-risk-your-farm

Basics of cover cropping. (n.d.). Organic Grow School. https://organicgrowersschool.org/gardeners/library/basics-of-cover-cropping/

Best cash crops for small farms. (2019, September 9). Farmers Weekly. https://www.fwi.co.uk/business/business-management/best-cash-crops-for-small-farms

Bonner, M. (2019, March 28). *What types of crop insurance can you buy?* The Balance Small Business. https://www.thebalancesmb.com/what-is-crop-insurance-4178498

Buffer strips: Common sense conservation. (n.d.). Usda.gov. https://www.nrcs.usda.gov/wps/portal/nrcs/detail/national/home/?cid=nrcs143_023568

Campbell, L. (2021, January 17). *The modern farmer guide to buying seeds.* Modern Farmer. https://modernfarmer.com/2021/01/the-modern-farmer-guide-to-buying-seeds/

Casey. (2021, March 19). *50+ ESSENTIAL farming tools & equipment for a small farm in 2021.* Farmhacker. https://farmhacker.com/farming-tools/

Chait, J. (2019, November 20). *Organic farmland requirements.* The Balance Small Business. https://www.thebalancesmb.com/organic-farmland-requirements-2538086

College, S. (2017, November 29). Seed suppliers and seed catalogs for small farming. Treehugger. https://www.treehugger.com/small-farming-seed-suppliers-and-seed-catalogs-3016666

Dizon, A. (2019, August 1). *20 Most Profitable Small Farm Ideas in 2019.* Fit Small Business. https://fitsmallbusiness.com/profitable-small-farm-ideas/

Does a farm need insurance? (2020, July 20). Advantage Insurance Solutions. https://www.teamais.net/blog/does-a-farm-need-insurance/

Downey, L. (2020, December 13). *What is crop-hail insurance?* Investopedia. https://www.investopedia.com/terms/c/crophail-insurance.asp

Elferink, M., & Schierhorn, F. (2016, April 7). G*lobal demand for food is rising. Can we meet it?* Harvard Business Review. https://hbr.org/2016/04/global-demand-for-food-is-rising-can-we-meet-it

Farm and Dairy Staff. (2017, January 4). 5 tips for setting farm goals. Farm and Dairy. https://www.farmanddairy.com/top-stories/5-tips-for-setting-farm-goals/389099.html

First time farmer loan: 3 steps to a successful loan application. (n.d.). Upstart University. https://university.upstartfarmers.com/first-time-farmer-loan

Freedman, M. (2021, July 12). *How to qualify for an agricultural loan.* Business.com. https://www.business.com/articles/agricultural-loans/

Funding resources for farmers (loans/grants). (n.d.).
Beginning Farmers.
https://www.beginningfarmers.org/funding-resources/

Glenney, J. (2019, March 7). *Seed placement is key to ensure highest yield potential.* Farmtario.
https://farmtario.com/crops/seed-placement-is-key-to-ensure-highest-yield-potential/

Grants & Opportunities. (n.d.). Agricultural Marketing Service U.S. Department of Agriculture.
https://www.ams.usda.gov/services/grants

Gullickson, G. (2018, August 28). *11 tips for growing your farm.* Successful Farming.
https://www.agriculture.com/farm-management/11-tips-for-growing-your-farm

Hayes, A. (2021, March 21). *Business plans: The ins and outs.* Investopedia.
https://www.investopedia.com/terms/b/business-plan.asp

Iannotti, M. (2021, June 12). *Should you start your vegetable garden from seeds or seedlings?* The Spruce.
https://www.thespruce.com/vegetable-garden-seeds-or-seedlings-1403412

Johnson, J. K. (2017, April 19). *8 things to consider when buying a tractor.* Hobby Farms.
https://www.hobbyfarms.com/8-things-consider-buying-tractor/

Kunz, L. (2016, February). *You need to be passionate about farming.* Grain SA.
https://www.grainsa.co.za/you-need-to-be-passionate-about-farming

Law, T. J. (2021, June 10). *17 seriously inspiring mission and vision statement examples.* Oberlo.
https://www.oberlo.com/blog/inspiring-mission-vision-

statement-
examples#:~:text=%20For%20quick%20reference%2C
%20here%20are%2017%20examples,at%20a...%207%
20TED%3A%20Spread%20ideas.%20More%20

Macher, R. (2014a, December). All about crop rotation.
Grit. https://www.grit.com/farm-and-
garden/crops/crop-rotation-ze0z1412zcalt

Macher, R. (2014b, December 18). *Twelve ways to sell
your products.* Grit.com/. https://www.grit.com/farm-
and-garden/sell-your-products-ze0z1412zcalt

McEvoy, M. (2020, December 14). O*rganic 101: Five
steps to organic certification.* U.S. Department of
Agriculture.
https://www.usda.gov/media/blog/2012/10/10/organic-
101-five-steps-organic-certification

McKenzie, R. H. (2017, November 22). *Understanding the
effects of sunlight, temperature and precipitation.* Top
Crop Manager. https://www.topcropmanager.com/back-
to-basics-20879/

Munniksma, L. (2019, October 21). *Learn the names of
farm equipment & what you need.* Hobby Farms.
https://www.hobbyfarms.com/names-of-farm-
equipment-4/

O'Neil, T. (2021, February 5). *9 reasons you should make
compost at home.* Simplify Gardening.
https://www.youtube.com/watch?v=A_OATaBRUaI

Pendleton, E. (2019, April 9). *How to obtain grant money
to start a farm.* Chron.
https://smallbusiness.chron.com/obtain-grant-money-
start-farm-17862.html

Queck-Matzie, T. (2019, December 16). *Tillage options
for farmers.* Successful Farming.

https://www.agriculture.com/machinery/tillage/tillage-tips

Starre, V. (2021, July 16). *Cold composting: Step-by-Step guide.* Treehugger. https://www.treehugger.com/cold-composting-step-by-step-guide-5186100

Storey, A. (2017, June 23). *What every new farmer should know about farm debt.* Upstart University. https://university.upstartfarmers.com/blog/new-farmer-farm-debt

Suitable methods of tillage for the farm. (n.d.). Www.fao.org. http://www.fao.org/3/y5146e/y5146e08.htm

What is seed funding and its various types. (n.d.). Tavaga. https://tavaga.com/tavagapedia/seed-funding/

Wickison, M. (2021, July 8). *27 ways to make money from your small farm.* ToughNickel. https://toughnickel.com/self-employment/small-farms

Made in the USA
Columbia, SC
06 October 2021

46816944R00148